A MILE IN YOUR SHOES:

The Road to Self-Actualization Through Compassion

By John Lawrence Maerz

Lulu Publishing

www.Lulu.com

TABLE OF CONTENTS

Section 3:

The MECHANISMS of the MIND

Section 4:

METAPHYSICAL & META-PSYCHOLOGICAL CONSIDERATIONS

Section 5:

THE ROAD TO REBALANCE

Section 6:

COMPASSION & ITS IMPLEMENTATION

Section 7:

PSYCHOLOGICAL PERSPECTIVES & EXTREME REACTIONS

INTRODUCTION

Next to love, compassion is the most poorly defined and misunderstood feeling that a human can experience. Saying so will elicit agreement from almost everyone. To say that it is learned, however, will engender tremendous controversy, especially, from those who are *unfamiliar* with its experience. It's been my experience that those who *have* experienced it agree; it is learned.

For centuries our literature has promoted the expression of compassion as one of our highest human potentials, yet, even in its dictionary definition, it still is an extremely elusive concept to gain a comprehension of. Most of the definitions are nebulous at best. I contend that the *flavor* of its definition is a function of the level of awareness that the definer has accomplished. Additionally, the meaning of compassion encompasses a broader scope of perception than any one person can conceive of. This makes it different for everyone. Someone who operates within the parameters of their senses will have a much more limited scope for their meaning than someone who operates within the Gestalt of their intuition; the latter having many more subtleties within their sphere of perception to include. Hence, a definition from the perspective of the senses will prove to be much simpler to render than if from the matrix of intuition and its multi-dimensionally subtle layers. In this way, our feeling for compassion evolves in a process as we do; step by step as if slowly adding layers that broaden the scope of our awareness, depth and comprehension. Through this expanding of experience, compassion is learned.

Relative to spiritual practices, we might assume that religion would have compassion "cornered in the market." Currently, nothing could be further from the truth. The fact is, scriptures cannot give an ample description of what compassion is or how to apply it. To understand why we must take a look at how scriptures come about.

Often, the individual who becomes enlightened by *having* a "spiritual" or "peak" experience is not the one who writes about it. This is true of Jesus, Buddha, Krishna, Mohammed and a host of others who became enlightened while assisting others in their seeking. Those who followed these icons attempted to formulate a recipe for their own enlightenment and others by observing and recording the actions and words of the enlightened ones. Since the writers had not directly had a "peak" experience themselves, they could only describe the experience second hand. With insufficient intuition and no direct experiential feeling, they wrote what they *thought* the experience was comprised of. Needless to say, what was rendered was a mere skeleton devoid of the feeling, dimension and depth that would be present had they had the experience themselves. Consider the difficulty in attempting to describe the taste of an apple. Unless you've had the experience yourself, you would have nothing to reference the taste to in order to "recreate" the experience in someone else's perception. The description would be seriously lacking in the important qualities needed for its comprehension. Now let's return to compassion. Buddha talks about compassion but how can we comprehend the experience he talked about as it is described in the scriptures unless we have *tasted* the apple ourselves? (You may hypothesize why I used an apple if you wish. I think you should have no trouble with the analogous inference!)

In the same light, books like the Bible, the Koran, the Talmud and other "word of God" scriptures are *written by people* who all have had their own impressions about what they've heard and seen from within the parameters of their own individually limited awarenesses and understandings. Yet, we still *literally* interpret these scriptures and are puzzled and confused as to why we find ourselves tangled with so many contradictory perspectives. To illustrate a point; what happens when we play telephone? Is the beginning statement the same as the last? Why would scriptures be any different?

Let me summarize what we've established thus far. First, compassion can only be nebulously defined at best due to the different dimensions of comprehension needed for its recognition. Second, compassion can be described by someone who has had the experience but the perception of the person hearing the description will alter it to fit their own level of awareness and third, something is lost in the "translation" if we *haven't* had the experience ourselves and attempt to explain it to someone else (scripture).

In an effort to provide a basis for some of the terms that I will use, let me include the basic difference I have perceived between sympathy, empathy and compassion which are often erroneously used interchangeably. First, sympathy is an *intellectual* recognition of what someone may be feeling or encountering in a situation they've observed or have known about. In itself, it has no sense of feeling other than what might be imagined by the sympathizer. Second, in empathy a person will *actually experience* what another person is feeling *involuntarily*. Third, in compassion, a person will empathize what another is feeling but *voluntarily*. It will result in them taking some kind of action to assist in mitigating the empathized situation. I will go into these differences in much more detail in later sections but this will suffice for now to give you a general sense of how I will apply them.

To understand the evolution of compassion we must begin at a point in an individual's history where there is little or no awareness of the concept. This begins where the individual has not yet begun to look outside his own circumstances due to his total focus on his needs for survival. At this level, even curiosity doesn't enter the picture until his needs are, at the least, partially met.

The BASICS

WHAT ARE WE DEALING WITH?

In our physical world survival seems to be becoming more and more difficult. Paying bills, deciphering contracts, dealing with corporations, insurance companies, legal entities and even our friends and enemies consume more and more of our time, energy and resources. At the end of our day we find ourselves completely exhausted just from dealing with our daily world's demands leading to our survival. Economic entities know the pressure we face and use it by making it necessary for us to invest extra energy and time simply to regain and/or retain our entitlements as a consumer. The act of even attempting to contact those entities by telephone gobbles up our time and energy in the infamous land of "hold" while waiting for a customer service representative to speak to us with a barely understandable Indian or Asian accent while asking us if there is anything else they can "help" us with after they've flopped miserably by spouting their helplessness in handling our "requests." Yet, in the face of all this aggravation and more, it is expected that we will greet these people and circumstances with a smile, compassion, patience and tolerance; all the qualities that we feel we are *not* receiving from the world. If we become distraught or angry they become indignant insisting that there is something wrong with *our* character by our objecting to being abused even if we can validate our concerns. The mere act of objecting is made to seem unreasonable. To add insult to injury, when we *do not* object to the abuse and *do* exhibit the compassion, patience and tolerance, we are manipulated by those who view compassion as a weakness and use it to our liability. We begin to feel that we're damned if we do and damned if we don't.

Those of us who have developed a conscience and manners by learning to integrate humanistic values into our thinking as a result of conscientious parents, religious scriptures and quality literature find ourselves diametrically opposed to survival in this world if we stick to those values and act according to our conscience. Almost every act we perform aligning us with our conscience seems to inhibit the acquisition of what we need for our physical survival and comfort. At this point even *we* start to doubt the sanity of adhering to the compassionate lifestyle that we had been told would provide us with a happy and "righteous" life. This disparity between these two opposing perspectives, essentially, the "war" between values and money, compels us all to wander and compromise ourselves in the gray areas that exist between them. As a result, there always seems to be a nebulous sense of guilt and dissatisfaction in the simple act of living. Being aware of the anxiety and stress associated with being "caught between" these internally warring factions underlies a struggle where its effects force us to deal with the issue, consciously or not, just so we may maintain a sense of sanity in dealing with others. It affects our health, our relationships and even our ability to do a good job at work. What can we do to release this pressure? The answer lies, not so much in what we can do, but, in our ability to understand what we are dealing with enough to make a choice as to where we would like to stand.

WE ARE ALL ANIMALS

No matter whom we are or what our station in life is, one fact that is undeniable is that we all must work from within our animal nature. If you are human and live within a body, this is a fact. All of our instincts and tendencies yield to this influence in the interest of maintaining our survival and the perpetuation of our species. All of our literature alludes to this struggle but never fully acknowledges that this was, and still is, our nature of origin. The first contemporary academic acknowledgement that postulates the *dominance* of this influence of this can be found in the writings of Sigmund Freud as he describes the nature of the Id. According to Freud, this part of us seeks food, shelter, safety, pleasure and a consistency of their supply. Even as we have later evolved toward seeing ourselves as having a drive toward actualizing ourselves beyond our physical nature, food, shelter and safety are still acknowledged in the works of Abraham Maslow in the first two levels of a Hierarchy of Needs as physiological and safety needs. He hypothesizes that these two needs must be addressed before any other concerns can be considered. An analogous story would be that you can't teach a man philosophy until his belly is full.

If the animal nature within us deals with all issues and instincts concerning our survival, we can say that the drive toward food, safety, shelter and reproduction are instinctual, survival oriented and, perhaps, hormonally and genetically generated. Though pleasure is not included in the Hierarchy of Needs but *is* part of Freud's picture, I suggest that all pleasure is the reduction of the tension, in varying degrees, involved in maintaining our survival in all its myriads of physical expression. As an example we can cite the orgasm, defecation and sleep as containing varying degrees of this reduction and, hence, it's inducing of pleasure. Pleasure is a function of being self–*ish*. Unfortunately, in our unspoken standard for appropriate social behavior it is considered to be in bad taste to even admit that we would prefer pleasure at the expense of being altruistic and giving to our family and friends. We make the *appearance* of going to great lengths to promote the sacrificing of our own desires in favor of the needs of others. Our desire to reduce the stress and pressure of living in a physical body through the pursuit of pleasure is a basic animalistic impulse that we all possess but are reluctant to admit to others, or even ourselves, for fear of being "excommunicated" from our families and social groups and being labeled as being insensitive and ambivalent to the needs of others. In the light of common sense we have to ask ourselves why is it so necessary to *appear* to deny these basic human needs? This denial has the effect of making us *appear* as if we are separating ourselves from our animal nature. Where does this tendency come from?

The first attempt to disassociate us from our animal nature was attempted through the insistence of our religious communities, ancient and contemporary, that we are separate, above or better than this nature and that to admit its presence in our constitution represented a diminishing of our spiritual value.

This insistence exemplifies the psychological defense mechanism of denial and creates within us what is referred to by C.C. Jung as our *Shadow*. The *Shadow* can simply be defined as our innate or developed qualities that we feel are unacceptable to the people or groups of people we wish to be associated with and, hence, repress those characteristics while projecting them on groups we wish to *disassociate* ourselves from. These people then become the scapegoats for our perceived inadequacies. This dynamic is one of the major causes of advancing neurosis and, in the worst extreme, schizophrenia that plagues us in our attempt to lead peaceful and contented lives. A beautiful expansion on this schism of perspective can be found in the "Divided Self" by R. D. Laing where he holds that in order to effectively treat emotional issues we must first put ourselves into the "head space" of those dealing with issues before we can fully comprehend the Gestalt of what they're faced with. In this way we can see that it is not only the actual issues that must be dealt with but, also, *perceived* inadequacies thereby necessitating the importance of comprehending a dimension that might otherwise go unnoticed. This then allows us to know how to fully approach the issues we're faced with on all levels, including what's been repressed, in order to regain balance by releasing and resurfacing the *Shadow* to our waking awareness.

To suppress the animal urges that contradict our "balanced" socially accepted traditions might help us to cohabitate with others but to deny those urges can have disastrous effects. Most of the current violence in our world is due to the repression, suppression, restriction and denial of the needs and desires that we *publicly* denounce as unreasonable, irrational, unfair and illegitimate but *privately* wish were our due. Our need for approval, support (for survival) and acceptance from the dominant group in power prevents us from acknowledging this disparity openly and publicly. Acknowledging the inappropriateness of its exposure or expression has been drilled into our subconscious by those we have learned expect our support form. In this light we can see that the repression of our animal nature becomes a tremendous vehicle for manipulating the rationing of our needs for survival. In a sense, this constitutes a form of emotional blackmail by those in power. But, this digresses into a much broader perspective than I prefer to deal with at this point without examining some of the fundamental concepts that provide a foundation for this dynamic energy to progress. In order to develop an understanding of compassion we must look at the quality of perception that it is founded upon. The ability to express compassion is founded upon the dynamics of empathy for which we, potentially, all have the capacity for its use and perception. The next step, then, is to build our understanding of empathy and how it works. Let's move on.

WHAT IS EMPATHY and HOW DOES IT WORK?

Empathy is the quality of, literally, experiencing what another person is feeling. This simple statement will engender an emphatic rejection from the scientific community, an agnostic or "standoffish" response from the psychological community and a tentative agreement from the metaphysical community. So, before we move on I'd like to offer some food for thought in the way of theories for consideration. Let's first consider the scientific approach.

To date there have been volumes of studies done dealing with the properties of energy and its laws, actions, fields and effects upon our physical world starting from the simple application of magnetic force all the way to the elusive qualities of gravity and quantum mechanics. To the mathematician and physician my presumptions will seem severely lacking in tangible evidence and certainly stretch theory to the breaking point much like a strand of pearls. However, even in the face of such disbelief I will still present my perspective for I think future research will *slowly* fill in the blanks over time verifying my contentions.

In recent years bioelectromagnetism has become a commonly accepted aspect inherent in all living creatures. The gamut runs all the way from use of the magnetic field in the migration of birds to the defense mechanism of eels emitting an electric field outside their bodies to ward off predators. Even in human biology not only do we acknowledge the change of an electrochemical charge occurring in the synapse of a nerve transmission but we have measured changes in the brain's electromagnetic states through the use of electroencephalography (EEG) and functional magnetic resonance imaging (fMRI). If you think that we are immune to any kind of energy short of electrical shock through physical contact, you might then ask yourself what happens when we're exposed to radiation? To microwaves? To cell phones? To overhead power lines? We have only begun to understand and acknowledge the effects of electromagnetic radiation on the human organism.

For the most part we, thus far, have only effectively measured our *receptivity* to changing electromagnetic environments but we have only recently begun to measure the fields that are *emitted* by all living things. The eel emits an electric field while the bat and whale emits sonar. How much of the eel's field is electric and how much is something else? How much of the whale's and bat's sonar is merely sound and how much is something else? What other animals also emit energy fields that we are unable to measure simply because we are unaware of them or don't have the tools to do so? Obviously, what an animal senses and projects into its environment is much more that just the sum of its five physical senses. Humans *were* just as sensitive but through the progressive denying our animal nature through yielding to the growing modern requirement for us to become "civilized," we have lost touch with the more subtle parts of our sensitivities; animal or otherwise. Were we able to consciously project an energy field beyond the physical at one time in our distant past? You might initially say no but consider the controversy generated in the wake of experiments dealing with telekinesis or moving objects with the mind (or whatever else is used). Can you still solidly say no? Newton said that for every action there is an opposite and equal reaction. This, essentially, defines polarity. In this light wouldn't it also make sense that we should be able to project what we are receptive to?

In recent years experiments were conducted where plants were wired to a modified EEG (electroencephalograph). A baseline was set and people were admitted to the room one by one. There was mostly no change with many people. But, when someone entered who acted angry and violent, the EEG of the plants registered an unmistakable response to that person. Apparently, the person emitted *something* that the plants were sensitive to. The experiment has been replicated many times since then.

How much more of a stretch is it to consider that a person walking into another person's space or "field" could alter what the other person feels beyond the senses such as heat and smell? Is the potential of a human emitting an energy field and having an effect on another person really that far removed from Faraday's discovery of *electromagnetic induction* where the movement of one energy field through another creates a change in it merely through its movement?

Science has acknowledged the projection of a heat field produced by a human but, as of yet, is hesitant to fully acknowledge the emission of an auric or energy field. Why? How tangible must tangible be? Attempting to prove that humans emit an energy field is much akin to spray-painting the invisible man. We can see the effects and the outline of what we are trying to measure but are unable to determine how or what to use to measure the field.

If what I have said thus far has only produced a consideration for the possibility that humans emit an energy field that can be recognized by others, then I have done what I intended to do for those of you who are strictly scientific. Maybe I've opened your mind? Next, let's address the psychological community.

The aspect of psychology that would best deal with empathy emanates from issues dealing with Social Cognitive Theory which states that "portions of an individual's knowledge acquisition can be directly related to observing others within the context of social interactions, experiences and outside media influences." (Wikipedia)

At first consideration you might say, "Wait a minute. It said observe, not feel." And you'd be right, but Social Cognitive Theory coupled with another development in neuroscience, first described in 1992 as *Mirror Neurons* (Ramachandran, 1992), would partially complete our explanation of how empathy might work from a neurological perspective.

In the eighties and nineties neurophysiologists at the University of Parma, Italy working with macaque monkeys that had their ventral premotor cortexes wired with electrodes, yielded the same readings whether they performed an action themselves or were just observing another monkey perform. When they later performed the same testing on humans, they found that in addition to the same brain regions utilized in the monkey, the mirroring properties in humans, measured with functional magnetic resonance imaging (fMRI) included a much wider network of neurons including the *inferior frontal cortex*, the *superior parietal lobe* and the *somatosensory cortex* which involves feeling (Gazzola et. al, 2006, 2009, Keiser et. al, 2010). In addition to observation, it was found that in both humans and monkeys the mirroring effect was also present as a reaction to sound (Kohler et. al, 2002).

The key component to the mirroring effect is that it seems to happen *involuntarily* through sight and sound. At this point we would now have to ask is it solely a function of sight and sound or does it occur in all the senses and, more poignantly, does it also occur in dimensions we have yet to discover and *attempt* to measure as with an electromagnetic field? Remember Faraday's electromagnetic induction? There is a very large difference in the measurable tangibility between energy and matter. So far we have only been able to measure energy as it affects something in the physical world. At what point does the potential for measurement cease to be a practicality?

You might say that this is all circumstantial, but, if enough circumstantial factors point to the same conclusion, is it really that hard to accept the potential for an "unproven" concept to be in play? In some circles science calls this a hypothesis!

Lastly, to the metaphysical community empathy has been long accepted as a fact of life. I used the word tentative relating to their agreement in their definition and acceptance of empathy in the metaphysical community, not because validation is needed, but, because it is the understanding of *what it is* that is needed. Those who *do* understand simply accept the fact that an individual will naturally be able to feel what another feels without having to exert any effort but, perhaps stressing a bit having to cope with the consequences of what they do. There are also those who are in the field as neophytes, sometimes longer, aware that they *should* feel *something* as part of the New Age movement, which they consider themselves part of, but as of yet, have no clue as to *what* they're feeling, where it's coming from or how to cope with it. For those who do *and* those who don't, the metaphysical field holds a very strong challenging and unspoken requirement concerning mastering empathy if they are to remain invested and competent in the field.

So, having offered some food for thought for those who are scientifically oriented, those who are psychologically oriented and to those who work within the metaphysical fields, let's move on to a more detailed explanation of its origins and what I believe is going on.

The English word, *empathy*, originated from the Greek word *empatheia*. This word in turn derives from *pathos* meaning passion or suffering. Two Germans, Herman Lotze and Robert Vischer, molded the word to *Einfühlung*, or "feeling into," to reflect a similar meaning. In 1909 E.B. Titchner translated the German word "*empathie*" into the now known English term *empathy*. According to our current dictionary definitions and origins, the Greek *Pathos* is defined as *feeling*. *Em-* has its root in *en-* which is *in* or *take in*.

Previously, I had alluded to the possibility that *empathy* can be perceived in two ways; *voluntarily* or *involuntarily*. Let's look at *voluntarily* first.

If we have lived through a challenge or a situation, have an awareness of its implications and have come to terms with it in a way where it is healthily integrated it into our life's journey, we will be more willing to allow ourselves to experience similar feelings as generated by another. In this case we might say that we would be more willing to "tune in" or allow a resonance to that person's feelings because we have a conscious familiarity with their type of experience. We should note here that resonance is a "re-sounding" similar to an echo according to the dictionary. As an example, we can compare the vibrations of a room full of different pitched tuning forks. As we strike one fork, all the forks *of the same pitch* in the room will begin vibrating. Those that aren't of the same pitch will not vibrate. If they are a harmonic of the fork's frequency, that is having, a slight similarity, they would vibrate but at a much lower intensity. As a result, our having a familiarity or similarity of experience to another's, we would resonate with them and have less resistance to vibrating at their "pitch." If the feelings were of joy, we could certainly understand that willingness. If they were of pain, we could at the least say that the familiarity of our having dealt with them, and hopefully, come to terms with their consequences, would make us less likely to be afraid of them enough for us to push them away. The key to empathizing voluntarily, then, is through a familiarity with, awareness of and a self confidence in having experienced another person's similar challenge or situation and having accepted or come to terms with its consequences *consciously*. The voluntary perception, then, appears to be a relatively easy circumstance to navigate.

Perceiving empathy *involuntarily*, however, is a different kettle of fish. If we resonate with another person while they are going through a challenge or situation that we have been through, are *unaware* of our difficulty in dealing with that situation and have not accepted or come to terms with its consequences, especially if it's a painful one, we will find those feelings uncomfortable in the least and intolerable at the most. We would also tend to deny and bury those feelings and avoid the person who is generating them. The key here is that, even in our attempts toward pushing them away, we will *still* experience them because we have been through a similar situation and will resonate with them unconsciously by virtue of having become sensitive and receptive to the same type of experience. Ironically, the more we resist that person and their feelings, the more we will tend to attract them *and* others with the same experience. As our resistance seems to create a polarization to the feeling, its energetic opposite is called to us from the universe in an attempt to rebalance or neutralize it.

So, to recap; if we've gone through a similar challenge or situation we *will experience* what the other person feels, willingly or not due to our tendency to resonate with their situation. If we are *unaware* of our participation and/or have *NOT* come to terms with the challenge within ourselves, we will tend to shun or avoid the person that generates those feelings so as not to feel similar pain. This may also occur on an unconscious level where we just don't feel comfortable around another person but we can't quite understand why and are not aware that we are feeling their pain. Paradoxically, we will also assume, unconsciously of course, that the feelings we "pick up" from that person are our own. In the same vein, we will gravitate toward the person who feels joy and, similarly, not understanding that resonance either. Unfortunately, the unconscious level is where the majority of us seem to resonate with each other.

So far, there are two "universal" dynamics in play in the above explanation. The first is that "Likes attracts like." We have often heard this, socially, in the old sayings such as, "Birds of a feather flock together" and "Water seeks its own level." We can see physical evidence of this example as we drop a mercury thermometer and shattering it on the floor. As the mercury "globules" roll around and closely approach each other, they tend to bunch up in one larger "glob" almost like they can't resist each other. They almost seem to pull at each other once they move into close enough proximity of each other's "orbit." We see social evidence of this when we witness writers grouping with writers and construction workers grouping with other construction workers. They group together because they share similar experiences and sense a shared rapport and perspective on life. The second dynamic is where opposites attract. This, at first glance, may seem contradictory but consider, in a social perspective, how often have we found two people together who share an exaggerated opposite in some aspect of their lives? For example, isn't someone who wastes money always found with a saver? Or, someone who talks excessively is found with the silent "thinker." Think not? Consider Felix Unger and Oscar Madison as the "Odd Couple." There's even some truth in Hollywood!

In the first dynamic, gravity seems to be the driving force. An asteroid moving through space will tend to "collect" debris to itself getting larger as it travels just like a street crowd is attracted together curious about the same circumstance. In the second dynamic, the universe seems to attempt to neutralize any extreme expression of a "charged" energy or physical manifestation by attracting its exact opposite. We might say each side of the polarity is "charged" against its polar opposite. In physics we call this action a movement toward *entropy* where anything distinctly different attracts its opposite tending to neutralize the differences and falling back into a homogeneity or an inert state. We can go farther out in our explanation by metaphysically comparing the tendency to attract or reunite as part of our tendency toward *evolution* and the tendency to discriminate or create difference as a tendency toward *involution*. This is, perhaps, something to contemplate or meditate upon. For those of you tending to cringe at the use of the word *metaphysical*, just relate to it as a condition that's just beyond the physical or as a hypothetic proposal. Most people seem to have a basic understanding of the word evolution and, metaphysically or otherwise, its meanings seem to be, universally, pretty similar.

SOME TERMS TO CONSIDER

It's extremely important that we have a clear understanding of what level of awareness is present when discussing empathy. Please note that when I speak of *empathizing*, I am simply referring to the act of resonating with or "taking in" and experiencing another's feelings. No awareness is implied. When I speak of *perceiving*, I am referring to being aware that we're feeling *something* but have yet to discriminate what the feeling is. When I speak of *recognizing*, I'm specifying that we have awareness as to whether that feeling is joy, sadness, apathy, etc.

WHAT'S THE DIFFERENCE BETWEEN EMPATHY AND SYMPATHY?

Sympathy is where we feel *for* another person while they're going through a situation rather than actually *experiencing* what they're feeling. This occurs when we haven't had the same challenge in our life but we do recognize that it *is* difficult for that person and that it would also be so for us if we were to go through the same circumstance. In this there is a quality of detachment in being one who *observes* the experience rather than the one who goes through it. Additionally, sympathy *cannot* occur in someone who is self absorbed. We *must* be paying attention to what is going on outside of our own sphere of experience. We must, also, possess a partial quality of selflessness or, at the least, the ability and a tendency to have consideration for someone other than ourselves. Sympathy, as it differs from empathy, is more of a *mental* quality through observing and attempting to imagine what the feeling might be like.

In empathy we *actually experience* the effects of what another person is going through. Notice I said the effects. That means we will have a nebulous feeling of pain, joy, anger, sadness, agitation, anticipation, peace or any other feeling common to us humans. As a human it is in our animal nature to have a continuously active internal radar. We can see (feel) a "blip" on the screen but, yet, might not be able to make out the details surrounding it. The fact that empathy *occurs* involuntarily and is *perceived* either voluntarily or involuntarily means that we *will* feel what we empathize whether we wish to or not. If we are *not aware* when this is happening, and most of us aren't, we will tend to think that what we're experiencing is of our own generation. As an example; if we walk into a room where people were previously arguing and then left, we will feel the anger and perhaps act on the feeling by being angry with others. Most of us will tend to assume that this anger is of our own making but can't quite understand what the feeling actually came from. To many with sensitivity and awareness, the emotional "residue" left in the room is tangible. In this way, there is truth in the statement often made that "the tension was so thick that you could cut it with a knife." Most of us do not even recognize that we feel angry and just react by wanting to leave or act on the feeling by being angry at someone else almost immediately after empathizing. It's much like having grabbed a hot potato and frantically searching for a place to drop it. Eventually, the urge to act will diminish over time as we empathize other feelings that "take up the space." Some of us who are aware of the feeling will recognize the anger and *still* act on it or want to leave. Still others of us will perceive it and recognize it as *not* being of our own making and refrain from acting on it or simply decide to leave the space. Regardless of which level we are on or how we act, we will still sense the feeling *involuntarily* and feel an urge to action. The action we take depends on the level of maturity and awareness that we've developed thus far.

I'd like to note here that I believe *everyone* has this radar like sensitivity. Part of the maturing of our awareness is becoming conscious of what we sense and learning to recognize when it is self generated and when it is not. The fact that we attract what we project augments the importance of the need for us to learn to master this dynamic so as to become clear and accountable for, not reactive to, our own "emissions" and be able to disarm the cloaking effect produced by our lack of awareness. This is an *extremely* important step toward enabling us to be able to work with empathy consciously. If we don't, the unconsciousness of this ability becomes a place of exposure and susceptibility to coercion from others and a major tool for their ability to manipulate us.

WHAT PART DOES EMPATHY PLAY IN ADDICTION?

Another important note; some of us who, generally, are *not* aware of our tendency to empathize and, as such, intensely feel the pain and stress of others unconsciously, tend to feel that *we* are unable to cope. We then find ways of deadening our senses so it appears to us that the feelings have been eradicated. I believe that this capacity is one of the major contributors to the problem of addiction. If we deluge ourselves with addictive experiences resulting in euphoria, such as drugs, alcohol, food, sex and more, the empathetic feelings are overwhelmed and obscured temporarily by the addictive influence. We *feel* we have escaped their torture. Essentially, what we feel as euphoria is merely the relief of pain for the period of time that their masking effects last. Unfortunately, there is always the "morning after" where what we avoided returns with a full intensity. Eventually, what we used to obscure the pain no longer has the potency required to overcome the stress and we have to "up the dosage" to gain the same results. Eventually, the addictive effects and their acquisition produce more pain and stress than the empathic feelings they were "designed" to obscure. This dynamic relationship between empathy and addictions will be covered more in depth later. Let's continue with discussing our understanding of empathy.

ORIGINS

SEQUENTIAL PROGRESSION OF AWARENESS

Our empathic sensitivity can be a blessing or a curse depending on our level of awareness and our prior development and experience in dealing with it. The effects of its occurrence are inescapable and can either be consciously diminished or augmented through understanding and awareness. Yet, empathy seems extremely nebulous and difficult to define with any degree of specificity. I will attempt to lay out a framework depicting sequential states of awareness relative to its evolution toward compassion. Please be advised that the left framework relates *solely to undesirable feelings* perceived through empathy. Generally, pleasing feelings are accepted and are rejected only in rare circumstances. Movement toward pleasing feeling is almost a given whether conscious or not.

No sensitivity and no awareness.	
Anxious and uncomfortable but not aware of feeling so. Exhibits a "knee jerk" reaction with a lack of awareness of doing so.	
Anxious and uncomfortable *with* an awareness of feeling so (A&U w/A of feeling so). Still exhibits a "knee jerk" reaction with a lack of awareness of doing so.	
(A&U w/A of feeling so). Exhibits a "knee jerk" reaction *with* an awareness of doing so.	
(Crossroads for choosing method of coping – Left column is "pushing the river" and right column is "going with the flow.")	
Consciously or unconsciously *obsesses and distracts* with activities in order to cloak the anxious and uncomfortable feelings.	(A&U w/A of feeling so) Possesses enough awareness of their reactivity to *choose the type of reaction* to exhibit.
Feels anxious and uncomfortable no longer with the awareness of feeling so. *Drawn to substances that deaden the senses* masking and suppressing the anxiety and uncomfortablility.	(A&U w/A of feeling so). Aware and detached enough to recognize that they can *choose to react or not.*
As tolerance level is reached, the substance is no longer at an effective enough intensity to deaden the senses. Anxiety & uncomfortablility "bleed through." Increasing the dosage only serves to increase the tolerance level thereby spiraling the resurfacing anxiety	(A&U w/A of feeling so). Aware and detached enough to recognize that they can *choose to remove themselves from the circumstances creating the stress and/or plan prevention for future involvements.*

& uncomfortablility sooner and sooner.	
Discomfort becomes intolerable. The desire for oblivion and suicide is considered.	(A&U w/A of feeling so). Aware and detached enough to ask *what is the cause* of these feelings?
	(A&U w/A of feeling so). Aware and detached enough to ask could it be that they might *be "in sync"* with the feelings of someone else?
	(A&U w/A of feeling so). Aware and detached enough to accept the possibility that they may be *tuning into someone else's feelings* and considering the possibility that what they are feeling *might not be of their own making.*
	Aware and detached enough to ask if they are doing or contributing something that *enables their receptivity* to someone else's feelings.
	Aware and detached enough to ask if their action somehow *fosters the other person's feelings and emissions.*
	Aware and detached enough to ask if they can somehow *alter or morph what the other person is feeling and emitting.*

In the chart preceding I have arranged levels of awareness in a sequential fashion in order to ease the complexity with which we must deal as we determine where someone might be in their progressive growth and mastery over their empathized feelings. Each sequential level on the "going with the flow" side adds a subtle but building change that marks the difference between each and promotes a gradual release or "thinning" of the cloaking effect that the lack of awareness seems to produce as we move in the direction from non-sensitivity to becoming progressively more sensitive. The "going with the flow" movement might be equivalent to *evolution* and comparable to the sculptor who starts with a large piece of marble and slowly chipping away, piece by piece, gradually exposing and increasing the clarity of his creation. Moving in the "pushing the river" sequence might be equivalent to *involution* and comparable to that sculptor slowly covering up or "cloaking" his sculpture with plaster of Paris so as to obscure the recognition of what lies beneath.

EMPATHY IS THE FOUNDATION FOR COMPASSION

Empathy can be defined as experiencing the effects of what another person feels and emits. What we "take in" can range from our being totally unconscious to the effects all the way to being totally aware of what we're receiving and where it is coming from. We can compare this in a physical way to walking through a cloud of perfume. Some of it "sticks to us" as we pass, more permeates us as we remain in the space while, all the while, we may or may not be aware of who has it on or even that we smell it. Like a scent we know that our experiencing or "taking in" of feelings also occurs involuntarily or whether we wish it or not simply by virtue of passing through or being in someone else's space through the principle of electromagnetic induction. It is important to reiterate that *empathy occurs involuntarily*. The fact that we may or may not be aware of its effects *has no bearing on whether we are receptive to it or not*. The next step is crucial to employing compassion. *We must be fully aware of what we are "taking in," where it is coming from and willing to do something about it.* Compassion, then, is the ability and willingness to act on what is empathized. It is *extremely* important to understand that compassion is *not possible* until empathy is first felt, recognized and identified.

Empathy is the mother of compassion. The first step toward compassion, then, is to recognize when our empathy is operating. The second step is to gain control and an awareness over our responses to it and the third is to put it into action as a result of our own volition. You might say that compassion is an empathy with conscious awareness, direction and volition.

COMPASSION AS RELATED TO INTENTION & MOTIVATION

One of the most difficult factors to assess is the motivation for an act of compassion. The motivation employed may come from multiple intentions, often, all happening at the same time. In a simple projection, the individual may possess idealistic causes for their act but at the same time may covertly serve a physical, emotional or personal social need. For example, an act may be performed unbidden under the guise of assisting a person in need with no required "repayment," if we can call the expected return as such. But the individual may actually be putting emotional "money in the bank" so the recipient feels obliged to return some form of future "payoff." When two or more intentions are served, one or more of those intentions may be unconscious. For example, if an act is done for a friend, the conscious intention may be in line with a felt sense of altruism where the performer is doing something that they feel their friend is in need of as in introducing them to people who might have a positive effect on their career. The conscious intention may honestly be portrayed with no expectation of reward; however, an underlying script may be to insure the continued companionship with the friend. How far this underlying intention may be below the threshold of awareness will follow the same structure for building awareness as outlined in the chart for developing sequential levels of empathy as shown previously. The more aware the individual is aware of his or her own issues; the closer the motivations will be to consciousness. That same act may also be intended as a "repayment" to the friend felt as an unconscious obligation by the performer for acts done by the friend on their behalf. In either case, both combinations may be of varying degrees of urgency depending on the unconscious content and level of awareness.

The above action, motivation and payoff or repayment is between only two people. But suppose the act had an intention which could encourage a payoff or repayment from more than two people? In this way the explanation for the motivation may vary depending on the context of the quierent's social connections. Let's look at an example. Suppose Jack performs an act that serves the personal needs of the customer base of his company. An obvious and primary payoff would be that he was making points with his boss, Bob, by actualizing profits for the corporation through stepping in and taking the reigns of control from a fellow employee and improving on his effectiveness. This would certainly endear him to his boss and make raises and promotion more likely. But when Jack told his girlfriend Sally what he did, his emphasis would shift from the corporate profits to highlighting his male aggressiveness, machismo and his ability to provide for his woman thereby cultivating her attraction to him. Jack also has been cultivating a new girlfriend, Mary. But Mary's values lie in a different venue. Mary works toward improving the welfare of animals, children and anyone that she sees as having an underdog status. She has no interest in corporate profits or male machismo. Jack now highlights the benefits that he is providing to his customer base showing that he is concerned for their individual rights and welfare. Of course, Mary is then impressed with his altruism and encouraged to be more attracted to him.

In all three contexts, the act is the same but Jack's expressed intentions are different. Jack's intentions may be conscious, unconscious or in combination depending on how he has or hasn't dealt with his personal issues. The point is that as humans, we are not without ulterior motives, especially, if we hold perspectives of ourselves that do not contribute to a strong self concept. Our self concept is innately strong when there are no opinions about ourselves that must be repressed or hidden from the world. In other words, if we have an active *Shadow*, we, invariably, will have ulterior motives designed to compensate for any number of perceived inadequacies that we must hide from the world. Ideally, true compassion can only be expressed by those who have reintegrated their *Shadow* into their waking consciousness. All other acts of compassion are subject to motivational scrutiny.

THE SHADOW, SHAME, SELF CONCEPT & LOCUS of CONTROL

In order to understand the evolution of our motivation for compassion we must first explore mind's framework comprising the *Shadow*, how it comes to be and its need for reintegration into our consciousness before we can truly call an act compassionate. This perspective very closely parallels the concept of the *Inferiority Complex* postulated by Alfred Adler and the idea of *Original Sin* put forward by any of the Christian doctrines. Let's first look at the *Shadow*.

As previously described, the *Shadow* is comprised of our innate or developed qualities that we find are not acceptable to the people we wish to obtain support and recognition from. Initially, these are behaviors or qualities that our parents and immediate family members find disturbing or distasteful causing us to have love withdrawn, ridicule or any number of responses intended toward discouraging the unwanted patterns. This in turn produces a sense of *shame* when the unfavorable behavior is exhibited. As we progress in age and start to socialize, we begin to include other people and groups in our preference for acceptance while aligning ourselves with their preferences and values thereby denying and repressing the qualities that reflect on us badly in their eyes. As these qualities become repressed and incorporated into our subconscious, we begin to polarize them by strengthening their opposite traits through over-compensation developing inner tension. To diminish this tension we ascribe them to others through a process of *projection,* further distancing ourselves from them as they are pushed deeper into the subconscious. This becomes a vicious cycle and the qualities that are believed to be undesirable become more and more inaccessible to the consciousness of the individual. This repression contributes to a perceived unworthiness or shame on the part of the individual as these qualities are unconsciously and instinctively compensated for through projection so as to prevent them from being exposed and bringing public shame. This has devastating consequences to the self-concept of the individual and life long implications.

Everyone performs some kind of *Shadowing* activity since different behaviors and qualities are acceptable in some contextual situations and some are not in others. This is generally accepted and adapted to by most people simply in order to get along in life. The adaptations in themselves produce no debilitating or inhibiting behaviors of any consequence other than contributing to a natural state of shame informing them of their limits in common life situations. These begin as conscious discriminations but eventually become relegated to the subconscious as familiarity and daily practice make it no longer necessary to consciously focus on them. To further understand the effects of *shadowing* we must first examine shame in more detail.

There are two types of shame: healthy and toxic. *Healthy shame* is the emotion that occurs when we extend ourselves past our limits and are exposed in the eyes of others. However, if we are not cognizant of our act as a transgression, and this is extremely important, we are *unable* to feel shame. Shame is a *learned* response. So the feeling of shame occurs when we transgress past what we *know* or *feel* our limits to be. Those limits can be physical in nature. For example, if we know that if we are unable to lift five hundred pounds, yet, we have told others that we can and are put to the test and fail, we are embarrassed and exposed and, hence, feel shame. If the limits are moral, for example, stealing or extending ourselves past our acknowledged social status, and we are caught, we feel shame through being exposed as amoral. If we are *not* observed by or exposed to others as we stretch past our known and acknowledged limits, we instead, feel *guilt*. Again, like shame, we must be cognizant of transgressions past our limits. *Guilt*, then, is also learned. The important understanding to be had is that *healthy shame* is an emotional response by the transgressor for the *act* of knowingly transgressing past his limits and being exposed. Knowing the act is perceived as wrong; we commit the act, are exposed and then feel shame for our *action*. It is also important to note that whether the perceived limits for shame are real or imagined, the effects of the emotion will yield the same result. *Toxic shame* (Bradshaw, 1988) involves a very different focus. In *toxic shame* the transgressor commits the act, is exposed and then feels shame for his *character*. How can this occur? In this case the transgressor sees shame as a reflection of his *self-concept* due to past training occurring in situations when his view of himself was forming and his caretakers, either consciously or unconsciously, abused his dependency, allegiance and loyalty.

Essentially, the person regards *themselves* as being inappropriate, shameful or unacceptable. The caretaker has slowly and effectively convinced the child that there is something wrong with *them*. *(Toxic shame)* "is the experience of the self judging who we are against the image that significant adults in our childhood have given us through their actions, words and gestures. When we feel *(toxic)* shame, we see ourselves as having failed to live up to that fantasy image created for us." (Middleton-Moz, 1990)

For *toxic shame* to manifest, we need two factors to be in place. First, we need a boss or caretaker who has a diminished self-concept themselves acquired through their own history of shaming and, second, we need a child, adolescent or young adult who trusts his caretaker and/or boss while being susceptible to their opinion and judgment through desiring their love and approval. Simply put, *healthy shame* occurs when a caretaker or boss says, "You've done a *bad thing*." *Toxic shame* occurs when a caretaker or boss says, "You're a *bad person* because you've done a bad thing." There are many reasons why a caretaker or boss may choose to implant and perpetuate shame in their subordinates, most of which I will not go into here. But, suffice it to say, it is generally done to maintain power and control over the subordinate so their own *toxic shame* is not exposed by the child, adolescent or young adult whether done consciously or not. In a sense, the caretaker holds the perspective, either consciously or unconsciously, that the best defense is a good offense. Even so, *healthy shame* is necessary. It informs us of our limits. *Toxic shame* is not. It *produces* limits that are much more restrictive than need be leading to inhibited actions, desires and expressions. Obviously, the *toxic shame* will be much more difficult for a therapist to navigate their client's release from due to its involvement with their self-concept.

There is another dimension to shame needing to be clarified; the *internalization* of shame. When an individual extends himself past his known limits enough times and feels shame through his exposure, that emotion is paired in memory with the scene containing the act as a *bind*. "Sufficient and necessary repetitions of the particular *emotional* shame sequence will create an internalized linkage, or *bind*. This can be true for any set of *emotional* sequences. When the expressions of anger, distress, fear or excitement (any *emotion*) becomes associated with shame, later experiences of these *emotions* will activate the shame spontaneously by triggering the entire scene. Shame need no longer be activated. The particular *emotion* itself becomes bound by shame, its expression constricted." (Kaufman, 1989) *(Please Note: I have substituted the word* emotion *or* emotional *for the word* affect *which is commonly used in psychology as a descriptive term for emotion).*

When *healthy shame* is internalized, especially in the form of morals or social expectations, that *bind* becomes what is commonly called conscience (Scheff, 1995) and is usually *retained* in conscious memory. Barring other factors, the individual with a healthy self-concept views these social rules as *external* and having little impact on how they view themselves. They see their actions and self-concept independently of each other. When *toxic shame* becomes internalized the *bind* has much more intensity since it involves the individual's diminished character and resulting poor self-concept. If the experiences are particularly intense and prolonged, the conscious experience of the bound scene may become effectively erased through being repressed leaving only the emotion. It is believed that shame *internalization* is the principle mechanism producing *repression*. In this way, any continuous triggering of just the emotion will produce a freezing of movement, paralysis, a silencing of speech, irrationality and an immobilization of the self simply through the dynamic of the internalized *bind* (Kaufman, 1989) (Scheff, 1995).

Having used *shadowing* above in its broadest meaning as it relates to *healthy shame,* we know that it is undesirable to have *any* form of shame exposed. We all have our acknowledged and unacknowledged limits and prefer that these are not shared with the world, hence, we deny, hide or make light of any embarrassment or situation where our actions may be perceived as overextending our skills. *Shadowing*, in its more common application, refers to *toxic shame* as was coined by John Bradshaw, (Bradshaw, 1988). This type of shame evolves into a vicious cycle damaging the child's self-concept and creating an approach to life which ultimately inhibits any action that might be *perceived* as having the possibility of resulting in feeling shame. In short, it undermines any action that might risk shame, embarrassment or ridicule. This perspective is the essence of an *inferiority complex*; that is, essentially, feeling that there is something inherently wrong or unacceptable about the self resulting in the minimizing of any effort put toward goals or objectives by the individual.

The rearing of children finds them in situations where they must depend on their parents or caretakers to provide all that they need to survive and stay safe while learning to be competent in handling life's issues. They begin to realize that they, usually due to their age and size, are unequal to the task of doing this themselves. "Since all children must grow up surrounded by adults, they are predisposed to consider themselves as small, weak and incapable of living alone. They do not trust themselves even to do those simple tasks of which adults believe they are capable without mistakes and clumsiness" (Adler, A., 1927). Essentially, they see their parents as bigger, more knowledgeable and having the power to "make things happen" for them. Faced with this type of "competition," they can only perceive themselves as being inferior. Add to this actively demeaning, ridiculing or initially making them aware of their ineffectiveness, generated by their caretaker's immaturity or need to maintain control, puts them into the psychological perspective of approaching life from a position of lack. This will make them much more likely to inhibit their actions for fear of overextending themselves, thereby, drawing criticism and ridicule that results in feeling shame. This produces a belief in their *self-concept* that they are "less than" others. This is tremendously damaging their self image and spirals them into further covering up any evidence that may validate this new coerced but chosen belief about themselves.

Any diminishing of a self-concept usually leads to a need to compensate for what is felt to be lacking. This can show itself in one of two ways: retreating to living "beneath the radar" in a state of hiding or energizing the individual into investing a large amount of energy into attempting to recover what they feel is lost or lacking. Depending on how intensely and frequently the feeling of inferiority has been implanted will often be telling as to how far the attempted compensation will go. With very intense diminishing, the compensation will often go well past the point of simply rebalancing the self-concept. Again, this compensation can drive the individual further into hiding or further out into the world to prove their belief about themselves as being wrong. Those that are driven further into hiding emit a sense of having been "beaten" into submission. They will often diminish themselves in the eyes of others so as not to attract attention to themselves for fear of having their perceived inadequacies discovered. Those that move "outward" approach the task by painting themselves in an extraordinarily positive light almost as if they are fighting a "Jihad" or holy war. These are the people that we find go well past a simple conversing about their qualities and observations to obsessively overemphasizing them to the degree that we start to feel badgered. These people must feel a frustration and belief that they will be unable to produce a competent image of themselves in the eyes of others unless they do so. "When the feeling of inferiority is intensified to the degree that children fear that they will never be able to overcome their weakness, the danger arises that in striving for compensation they will not be satisfied with a simple restoration of the balance of power. They will seek to tip the scales in the opposite direction. In such cases the striving for power and dominance may become so exaggerated and intensified that it must be called pathological, and the ordinary relationships of life will never be satisfactory" (Adler, A., 1927). It also becomes apparent when dealing with people of this perspective that they are unable to be receptive to others except to listen for cues on how best to promote themselves while keeping their sense of shame well hidden and covered. Their push for dominance takes on a quality of urgency almost to the point of desperation. "Individuals with a pathological power-drive seek to secure their position in life with extraordinary efforts, exceptional haste and impatience, with violent impulses, and all without the slightest consideration for others" (Adler, A., 1927). (This will be covered in Section 7 "Extreme Reactions").

Both, those who live "beneath the radar" and those who over compensate outwardly, are dealing with the same issue but have different methods of coping with their perception of their diminished selves. Why do some people go "all out" and others go into hiding? My belief is that those who go into hiding have been pushed well past their ability to cope and, in a sense, have had their "spirit broken." As a result, they have given up. All they see is hopelessness in attempting to prove their competency as the tide of demeaning and diminishing directed at them by their caretakers has been "tsunamic" in nature. The fear of retaliation, shame and punishment is overwhelming. Their belief about the world then develops in a way where they feel that they have no control over their life and that the world determines their course of fate. Fear and protection from the exposure of their perceived shameful self becomes their motivating factor in life. Their shame becomes their punishment. In psychological terms these people have developed an *external locus of control*. That is, they believe that events in their lives are controlled by external factors and other people. They move through life *reacting* to circumstances rather than approaching difficult situations from a sense of strength and competence. You might assume that since the people who retreat or self-diminish have an *external locus of control* that those who are outwardly directed would have an *internal locus of control*. I feel that this is *not* the case as those who are outwardly directed through overcompensation are still *reacting* to their perceived inadequacies in the eyes of others. Essentially, they are still *externally* motivated. Before we cover the *internal locus of control* we must look a bit more deeply and the dynamics involved in the *external locus of control* and the *Beta Point*.

EXTERNAL LOCUS of CONTROL & BETA POINT

At this point we can say that those who are *toxically shamed* into hiding **and** those who are *toxically shamed* into over compensating are *both* reacting to an external motivation making them subject to an *external locus of control*. The major difference between them is that the thrust of reaction created is either outwardly or inwardly directed, yet, the reaction is still a result of externally generated forces. We then have to ask two questions; first, what would make one person more susceptible to *reacting* to external forces than another and, second, which direction would they choose to focus that energy; inward or outward?

To answer the first question, whether they would be reactive or not, would depend on the intensity and duration of the shame applied, whether it is *toxic shame*, *healthy shame* or no shame at all and the person's sensitivity, resiliency and strength in keeping a solid self-concept throughout a "shame assault."

When a child is born they come into this world absent of shame (remember that it is learned), however, they do come in with a propensity toward a general proximity of one of the loci of controls, ostensibly, due to heredity, training, karmic residue and any other number of factors that might contribute to their perceptual capabilities, although they may not yet necessarily perceive which or why. The strength and direction (internal or external) of the *locus of control* that they "come in" with serves as a starting point for them to learn a directional attitude with shame. The type and extent of shame incorporated into their self-concept through learning is determined almost exclusively by their family, caretakers and teachers.

Please note that when I speak of *locus of control* that individuals are not totally either or. They exhibit preponderance toward one more than the other and the ratio between them will vary depending on the child's incoming preponderance and, sequentially, the intensity and duration of the shame applied or its opposite; encouragement or "self determinism," of which I will speak more of shortly. In short, we might say that someone who exhibits strong evidence of *toxic shaming* will be more external than internal in their *locus of control*. That is, they may be external 80% of the time and internal 20% of the time depending on which life circumstances get triggered and are related to the shame producing process. Others, who have not had such an intense application and duration of shame or maybe only had received reinforcement in certain areas of their life, may be externally motivated 55% of the time and internally 45% of the time. The point at which the 55% and 45% meet may be considered to be their personal balance point. No one is ever totally one or the other. They all exist in varying degrees of ratio and intensity and as their experience changes, so might this ratio. After all, aren't we all evolving toward the actualization of the self? The process could not be static if this were so.

At this point we're beginning to see that shame and *locus of control* are very tightly dependent on each other and that the ratio between which one is dominant and which one is not may change through life experience or assistance.

In a similar way that we could say that every person has their price, we could also say that everyone has their breaking point where a "shame assault" becomes so overwhelming that they literally give up directing their life circumstances and submit to the belief that the world, or more external than internal circumstances, now direct their life progress and direction. The "shame assault" has, essentially, bulldozed them into perceiving themselves as being more helpless and hopeless.

Some individuals will be able to sustain a more intense and concentrated "shame assault" than others. Many individuals are resilient enough and bounce back to their beginning beliefs contained in their self-concept of whether their world is controlled by internal or external circumstances. Some are not so lucky. With an extended assault, some are pushed to their furthest point of resistance where they no longer have the strength or energy to resist the onslaught any longer and "let go" of control over their life circumstances and abandon any effort to do so. This point of breaking or letting go I call the *Beta Point* and it is as individual as a finger print in that each person has a specific combination of factors that contribute to the "setting" of their point.

Each individual's *Beta point,* or tipping point, will be found at a different shame intensity threshold point depending on their sensitivity, strength and resiliency. It will be at this point that the individual will decide as to whether they are motivated by an *external* or *internal locus of control.* So we now have a balance point *and* a tipping point at some distance from the balance point, different in each person depending on their stamina, that will be the threshold for a change to a more *internal* or *external locus of control* depending on the direction, strength and duration of either a "shame assault" or an encouraged "self determinism" applied by the parents, caretakers or teachers.

I would caution the reader, at this point, that because the combination of *toxic shame* and *external locus of control* would point an individual into a life focus that might be less than idealistic, not to assume that the remedy for the perceived difficulties might be an exclusive culturing of an *internal locus of control.* Even though it may appear that it would prove to be the type of energy to "set things right" it too is fraught with difficulties and contributing factors that don't always result in the best perspectives.

INTERNAL LOCUS of CONTROL
& SHAME FREE SELF CONCEPTS

Most of us long for more encouragement and support from those who have raised us. But suppose you are one of those "lucky" children who have received unconditional support from your parents, caretakers or teachers? Does that really put you in a better place with your developing self concept? Consider little "Joey" as I will call him. Joey has been raised in a totally permissive environment and never left wanting for any material or emotional desire. Everyone has "bent over backwards" to make certain that all his needs and desires are met. He has never experienced the restriction of rules, requirements or responsibilities. He has come to expect that the world will produce everything that he might need for his pleasure and amusement. For him there was no struggle, no challenge, no sense of earning or need to exert himself in any way to acquire his amusements and pleasures. When his parents were both killed in a car crash, he was sent to live with his aunt and uncle who were very hard working and responsible people. Since his aunt and uncle hadn't seen him since he was born, they naturally expected that he would at the least be able to take care of the simplest responsibilities such as personal hygiene, keeping his room reasonably clean, respecting their privacy and possessions, have at least a rudimentary set of manners and would be willing and able to listen when he was instructed on issues concerning his dealings with the world as he was still a child. To his aunt's and uncle's horror, it quickly became apparent that little Joey was neither able nor willing to do any of those things. Frequently, he had temper tantrums when he didn't received what he demanded, left a trail of garbage throughout the house, and broke things when they were either in his way or didn't perform as required and showing no remorse when he was confronted. He was totally disrespectful and verbally abusive to his aunt and uncle for any admonishments and any ability to listen and respond to his aunt and uncle were totally absent unless they capitulated to his demands. The found that they had taken in a little monster, and that it would probably take years, if at all, to "retrain" him into behaving "civilly." Needless to say, their task would be a daunting one of which intense therapy would have to be an integral part.

So, what had happened to little Joey's self concept? Simple; he was never indoctrinated to *healthy shame* which shows us the limits to which we can extend ourselves into our environment. His sense of self importance and omnipotence had exploded exponentially. Having never been exposed to the needs of others, he has no concept of what anyone else is feeling or thinking. Empathy, let alone compassion or shame, are foreign concepts to him. (Remember, though, that empathy is involuntary and may also be responsible for contributing to his tantrums). Given this, he has no need of manners, consideration or even to listen. Essentially, little Joey was raised with no sensitivity other than to his own needs and desires and would probably be surprised to find that others *actually have* feelings and thoughts. However, why would he care if he was already getting everything he needs or wants? For someone who could be totally self sufficient, there might not be a necessity for any of these skills or capabilities, however, when little Joey begins school, everyone, including him, will encounter staggering difficulties. His current perspective is such that everyone is supposed to respond to *his* demands. His *locus of control* is totally motivated internally. He believes that *he* runs the world he lives in. The only time that he is responsive to others is when his needs are not met. The key to his attitude and behavior rests in the fact that somehow the environment and the significant people who raised him, whether through neglect or intention, have contributed to the elimination of any circumstances that might have allowed any room for his sensitivity to others to develop. The most discouraging part of his condition is that he will have to first be *untrained* before he can be *retrained*. Remember that shame, healthy or toxic, is learned. Meanwhile, he has a lot of "ground to make up" and a long road to achieve balance.

At this point I'd like to emphasize that others who have little shame are not of the extreme situation that little Joey is subject to; however, they still have a long way to go before compassion can be part of their emotional makeup. Both extremes, *toxic shame* and *no shame*, are equally distant from feeling, recognizing and utilizing compassion because of being subject to the necessity of compensation or having an extreme absence of sensitivity to others. Both need to find a path back toward some semblance of balance between the two before they can begin to have their sensitivity register at a place where they can at least recognize the potential to utilize it. In the case of the *toxically shamed* individual, it is as if they are in a crowded room unable to hear a whisper. The roar of the conversation (inner shaming talk) is so overwhelmingly loud that it completely obscures the more subtle qualities of what needs to be perceived in order to properly gauge what is needed for another person. The person with *no shame*, essentially, doesn't even perceive others as people, let alone perceive what they might need or feel.

Following is a visual diagram that will add dimension to our understanding of the relationship between toxic shame and no shame.

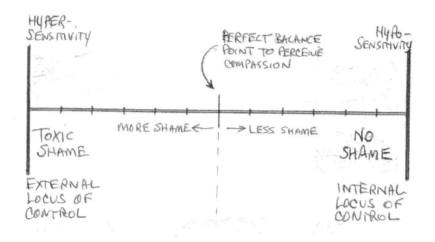

NARCISSISM: SHAME BASED or NOT?

Insensitivity to others and their plight is one of the hall marks of narcissism. Symptoms of narcissism can be described as egotism, vanity, conceit and some forms of selfishness. However, whether this insensitivity is shame based or not depends on one very important factor; is the individual egotistical, vain and conceited because he is compensating for perceived inadequacies or is the behavior due to having never learned personal limits or sensitivity to others and having nothing to compensate for? For the former example, there would be awareness on *some level,* even unconsciously, that their behavior is put on as a compensation. For the latter, there would be no awareness of being perceived by others as insensitive. In fact, that individual would believe that others' reluctance to concede to his wishes would make *them* insensitive!

The distinction between the two types, with a variation on the second, allows us to properly qualify when the *locus of control* for narcissistic behavior is external or internal. James Masterson divides the first example into two types: *closet narcissism* and *exhibitionist narcissism* (Masterson, J, 1993). Both of these types are compensatory and, due to learned personal limits and sensitivity to others, follow an external *locus of control.* Their difference is that the *closet narcissist* is driven into hiding or drops "below the radar" in order to prevent their shame from being discovered. The *exhibitionist narcissist* moves in an outward direction masking his shame by extolling his specialness to those that he feels may have perceived him as being inadequate. The second example has a variation where there has been *no* training or experience in sensitivity or personal limits that provides the basis for shame. Little Joey would be a primary example of this. This variation of the *exhibitionist narcissist* would be best attributed as having an *internal locus of control* and be considered pathological.

While the *closet narcissist's* primary defense for a feeling of inadequacy will be to compensate through modesty and self-deprecation, the *exhibitionist narcissist's* primary defense will be to either step up the assertion of the self's superiority or literally walk away in order to prevent any attempted diminishing of their projected self image through an external assault or comparison.

There are two exceptions to these classifications as there always are to every "blanket" classification. First, a form of *exhibitionist narcissism* that is developed *after* childhood is exemplified in a newly emerging celebrity who develops an inordinate amount of wealth and fame. As the celebrity develops this extended feeling of popularity and a growing devotion of fans, their sense of self begins to warp and develop a heightened and unreal sense of power and untouchability. "The lack of social norms, controls, and of people telling them how life really is, also makes these people believe they are invulnerable" (Crompton, C., 2007). They grow to feel that they are more important than anyone else and that they are above having to give courtesy or live by the rules of "ordinary" people. They progressively lose their sensitivity to the feelings and welfare of others. If they are able to totally blot out any trace of shame, they will follow an *internal locus of control.* If they have been unable to do so and are still aware of their learned sensitivity to others and personal limits on *some level,* they will be compensatory and follow an *external locus of control.* This type of narcissism is referred to as *Acquired Situational Narcissism* or ASN as per Robert B. Millman, professor of psychiatry at Cornell University. "Millman says that what happens to celebrities is that they get so used to people looking at them that they stop looking back at other people" (Compton, C., 2007). The defense mechanism utilized will be the same as mentioned previously. Second, little Joey was depicted as an extreme example of insensitivity in order to create an impression and mirrors the "blotting out" effect. It is highly unlikely for us to encounter anyone as he who has had every want and need answered as a child, thereby, creating an exhibitionist little "monster." These types of individuals will also be extremely rare as well as extremely pathological.

Obviously, most of us will have limited exposure to the exceptions so; hence, we will be less likely to experience cases of ASN or representatives of extreme pathology. However, relative to the prior two classifications, *closet* and *exhibitionist* (both having learned personal limits and sensitivity to others), we will have plenty of occasions to experience both as they relate to shame and their compensations. We must also understand that all the types need to be approached differently in order to bring them back into balance.

Narcissism, thus far, has been presented with many variations and any insensitivity in its extreme can most certainly be classified as pathological. However, with a lesser measure of insensitivity, we move down the scale toward balance. Yet, for a person to maintain a sense of autonomy in the face of others who may solicit excessive energy and time, a measure of "put on" insensitivity may become necessary for self preservation and personal balance. For those soliciting the energy and time, they may claim that the person being insensitive to them is behaving narcissistically. In this light, this may indeed be so. Andrew P. Morrison claims that, "in adults, a reasonable amount of healthy narcissism allows the individual's perception of his needs to be balanced in relation to others" (Morrison, P. 1997).

DEPRESSION, LEARNED HELPLESSNESS & TRAUMA

There are three other conditions which must be considered before we move on to understanding how compassion is allowed to develop. All of these are often codependent and destabilize the balance and awareness required to feel and use compassion. The key to how all of these conditions are exhibited is dependent on the individual's perception of how much control they believe themselves to have over their situations. They are strongly connected to our individual Beta Points. Let's first examine depression.

Depression has many faces in our current social structure. Next to our belief that other people and external circumstance prevent us from achieving "happiness," depression provides the most far reaching and insidious forms of *self generated* discouragement leaving us to be our own obstruction to the circumstances that we believe will produce "happiness." This *self generated* discouragement has its origins in the shame we have internalized. The degree to which our motivation toward action is dampened is proportional to the degree to which we feel shame, toxic or not. To understand this dynamic better, it would be prudent to first give some conventional and popular definitions of depression.

Wikipedia describes *depression* as "a state of low mood and aversion to activity that can affect a person's thoughts, behaviour, feelings and physical well-being. Depressed people may feel sad, anxious, empty, hopeless, helpless, worthless, guilty, irritable, or restless. They may lose interest in activities that once were pleasurable, experience loss of appetite or overeating, or problems concentrating, remembering details or making decisions; and may contemplate or attempt suicide."

The dictionary describes *depression* as "a state of feeling sad: dejection *(2)* : a psychoneurotic or psychotic disorder marked especially by sadness, inactivity, difficulty in thinking and concentration, a significant increase or decrease in appetite and time spent sleeping, feelings of dejection and hopelessness, and sometimes suicidal tendencies *(1)* : a reduction in activity, amount, quality, or force *(2)* : a lowering of vitality or functional activity."

The description from the DSM-IV-TR (Diagnostic and Statistical Manual of Mental Disorders) was much more difficult to pin down. The diagnoses changed depending on the combination of "symptoms", their duration, the part of life exhibited in, concurrent conditions, chronicity, intensity (observable) and many more factors. The practice of distinguishing between the diagnostic "labels" drops us in a miasma of conditions where their tendency toward overlapping severely blurs the conceptual understanding of the essential condition. One of the more general descriptions which will serve our purposes is that of a depressive personality disorder which is described as "a pervasive pattern of depressive cognitions and behaviors beginning by early adulthood and present in a variety of contexts, as indicated by five (or more) of the following: (1) usual mood is dominated by dejection, gloominess, cheerlessness, joylessness, unhappiness, (2) self-concept centers around beliefs of inadequacy, worthlessness, and low self esteem, (3) is critical, blaming, and derogatory toward self, (4) is brooding and given to worry, (5) is negativistic, critical, and judgmental toward others, (6) is pessimistic, (7) is prone to feeling guilty or remorseful." This classification is presented as criteria for further study on page 789.

To over-simplify any situation or condition usually has the effect of losing important dimensions that provide us with contextual understanding to the extent that we are able to see parallels to circumstances within our own lives. After all, we are a culture that thrives on the detail that allows us to "pigeon hole" or "label" any condition or situation so we either no longer have to apply any thought in order to take part in its usefulness or give ourselves permission to push it out of our awareness due to its believed "uselessness." This, I believe, is an important part of the western mind set diverting us from perceiving any issues or conditions as part of a Gestalt or from a holistic perspective allowing for seemingly contradictory, yet essential, components that contribute to understanding the situation's inter-dependent qualities and connective and effects. What I feel is more important, at least in this case, is to reveal the simple underlying dynamic that powers all depression; and that is the shutting down or diminishing the energy available for motivation through capturing it in a closed circuit "loop" that holds in place and perpetuates an irresolvable mental pattern or perspective.

For us to feel motivated, we must simply feel that there is the possibility and potential to move in a direction that will bring a desired payoff. That payoff could be a sense of satisfaction, accomplishment, belonging, pride or any other number of factors that we feel contributes to our well being. In some methods of thinking this would be described as having hope or, at the least, having a sense of anticipation or expectation that some effort or situation will yield results that will favor that sense of well being. This sense of well being is totally subjective by virtue of the fact that we must individually and personally perceive it as so. We can be told what a sense of well being is "supposed" to be but in the final analysis it is we who must decide what constitutes that feeling for us. That perception then leads to forming a core belief about ourselves and the world for the perspective of well being that we choose to invest in. The justification for that perspective will be based on the response that comes back from the world and what we choose to accept as valid proof of that reality. When an experience occurs that threatens that sense and conflicts with our chosen core beliefs, resistance and tension ensues. If we deny or refuse to acknowledge the conflicting experience or refuse to change or adjust to the changes that match the new, evolved form, we find ourselves in a closed loop where we feel pain due to our resistance to being attentive to the needed change in perspective and our sense of reality becomes distorted. *Toxic shame* and trauma are among those conflicting circumstances that challenge our core beliefs about ourselves.

When *toxic shame* or traumatic experiences begin to appear as if they are the *cause* of our current life circumstances, we begin to doubt the influence we feel we have over our lives. As *toxic shame* is allowed to progress more intensely and for longer periods of time, and with an increasing effect of the trauma, we begin to develop a sense of feeling overwhelmed and our motivation to act begins to waver. As the feeling progresses, our *locus of control* begins to shift. We feel less in control. We, eventually, pass through our *Beta Point* moving from an internal *locus of control* to an external one. We have now shifted from being proactive to reactive. Our core belief asserting that we can handle the world and determine our own fate has just shifted to feeling that we are more at the mercy of world causes and circumstance beyond our control. As we begin to feel more overwhelmed, our motivation to act on our own behalf diminishes and we begin to lose hope. This feeling of hopelessness encourages us to give up attempting to maintain or rebalance our lives more and more. As our giving up becomes more and more frequent, the energy we have been applying as a result of feeling that we *can* influence our lives slowly diminishes and eventually ceases by yielding to the newly forming belief that we *can't*. In short, if the experiences encouraging self reliance and self determination diminish and the experiences showing our decreasing influence in the world increases, our *locus of control* begins to move toward external. The more it moves toward external, the more we withdraw from exerting effort to effect change. We apply less and less effort (energy) and, if the changes in perspective are radical enough, we "shut down."

If these conflicting experiences occur in childhood, our core belief concerning our ability to have an influence on the world diminishes at an earlier age and before we've had an opportunity to set that core belief solidly within our self-concept. It is then more likely that we will decide that all life is reactive and, hence, operate more under an external *locus of control*. If the conflicting experiences occur in adulthood, our more extensive experience with life provides a broader sense of reference to draw on so we face a much better chance of regaining a proactive perspective and, hence, are able to operate under a more internal *locus of control*. Please remember that every human operates under a combined internal / external locus of control which is constantly shifting the point of their balance depending on the ratio between experiencing life as being internally or externally generated. For one person, they may experience life as being (20%) proactively generated or validating an internal *locus of control* while being (80%) responsive or reactive to external circumstances validating an external *locus of control*. The balance point will lie closer toward the right thereby showing a much larger component of reactively oriented beliefs (80%) than proactive (20%).

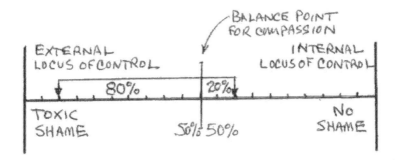

Another person may have (30%) of their experience validating an external *locus of control* and (70%) validating an internal *locus of control*. That would put their balance point further toward the left showing a larger portion (70%) of internally generated beliefs shown in the following diagram.

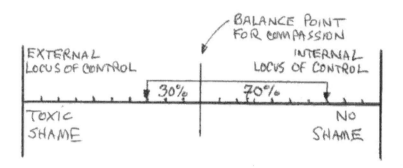

The ideal place of balance is, of course, (50%) by (50%), showing a balance of influences where the motivation to action shows no skewing toward either extreme. When the individual has neither a preoccupation nor a preference for validating their experience with either internal or external influences, the receptivity to more subtle forces or energies is awakened. This is much the same as being in a room which has suddenly become quiet enabling us to perceive the whispers beneath the prior noise threshold. It is only in this balanced frame of perception that compassion is able to thrive and grow. Please remember that internal and external may be defined from a static perspective in terms of their ratio to each other relative to their extremes but still operates dynamically.

Toxic shame and trauma have essentially the same effect in shifting our *Beta Point* but occur in different time schemes. *Toxic shame* occurs over a long period of time building an "escrow of evidence" much like a dam that is required to hold more and more water. Eventually, the dam bursts due to the overwhelming effect of too much water. Trauma occurs as if the dam receives the total volume beyond its capacity in one overwhelming occurrence.

As an example of *toxic shame*, we can consider a youth who has an adult or caretaker involved in his rearing who diminishes the youth's self-value and effectiveness by continually criticizing, embarrassing, competing with and invalidating any effort put forward by the youth. If we assume that the youth loves and respects his caretaker, he will be more likely to accept his caretaker's "opinion" of him has having more validity than his own. After all, at his age and lack of experience with the world, where has he had the opportunity to see life from a different perspective? Over a long period of time the treatment he receives slowly begins to show him that external circumstances have more say so and power over him than any effort that he can muster up on his own. Accordingly, his core beliefs form to reflect a reactive nature, that is, that the world determines who he is and what he can do. When an experience occurs that shows him that he has the potential for self reliance and self determination, say, he becomes proficient and effective in some skill and ability, his tendency will be to deny that skill and its potential because it runs contrary to his belief about himself established by his experience with his caretaker. The energy that would be applied to performing those effective skills becomes "corralled" and locked up in a closed mental loop reaffirming his "ineffectiveness." As more circumstances occur that run contrary to his core belief, the dam fills up and the pressure builds. The polarity between the two develops a stronger difference of potential. It now takes more and more energy to make sure the evidence conflicting with his perception of being ineffective remains repressed. Eventually, his ability to just simply function in everyday activities runs short of energy. He begins to stop putting effort into things like hygiene, diet, work, and friends and essentially, shuts down from participating in life because he no longer has the energy. He is now, what our culture would consider, depressed.

In a worse case scenario, our youth would unconsciously self sabotage any threat of becoming self reliant and self determinate in order to be certain that his self-concept would remain in tact to maintain a sense of security and being in control even though that sense is one of feeling diminished.

Since the belief about ineffectiveness has been established in the youth's childhood where he has seen no other perspective *and* due to the fact that he needs his caretaker for his survival and would, therefore, feel obligated to do nothing that would interfere with their relationship, the youth faces a very strong possibility that a reactive approach toward life circumstances will remain with him over the better part of his life. Had he been older before the move toward an external *locus of control* took place, he would have, at the least, had the possibility of originally having an internal *locus of control* to compare against and, therefore, an opportunity for choice. Additionally, for the caretaker to have a condescending attitude toward the youth, he would have had to have had is own issues contending with a diminished self-concept as trained by *his* caretaker. This would compare to what Adler would have called an *inferiority complex* and the old adage that the sins of the father are passed on to the son.

Before I move on to discussing *learned helplessness* I'd like to draw your attention to a scenario that will give depth and a sense of universality to the application of the *Beta Point* dynamic. If you remember, the *Beta Point* is where a shift takes place within an individual where he submits to a belief that his worldly expression and motivation to act changes from reactive to proactive or proactive to reactive.

We humans generally assume that an animal has less potential to think and in doing so we assume that their action comes from instinct (impulse) or is conditioned (reactive and trained). To see the connection, it will help to think of an animal being like a small child who has yet to develop the ability to think actions through to determine their consequences. Both the child and the animal will initially act according to their natural instinct (impulse).

Consider a stallion. The common assumption is that they are wild, unpredictable and need to be "tamed" if they are to be included in the human world of relations. The usual word used is domesticated. We would think the same of a caveman but we would call it civilized. Essentially, both are of the same intention; to make them relationally useful within our culture or society. To this end we would embark on a quest to cull or diminish the behavior that would cause problems for that usefulness. For the stallion, that would include training him to accept a bridle, a saddle and to obey commands that would avail his usefulness to his caretaker. The goal of this training, then, would be to coerce them into submitting to the direction or impulse of their caretaker. This would also include insuring the safety of the caretaker. This all seems "kosher" and within the limits of what we have come to expect within our society's structure. However, an old vernacular describes the process of training this stallion with much more color, directness and clarity than the customary way we describe it where we avoid disturbing images and inferences that mute the intensity of the act. In the past we have called it "breaking" the horse. More appropriately, it is closer to what we might call "breaking the spirit" of the horse. Horses have *Beta Points* also and, although it might not be a mental choice that the horse makes to attend more to external influences than to the natural balance that exists within them to be equally invested in both internal and external, the overall effect is the same; to push them more into a reactive behavior than a proactive one (if we can call it that).

Animals, as with humans, are born with a balance between responsiveness to external and internal influences. The internal influences are associated with impulse, expression and urge that come from our innate animal nature. The external influences are associated with our feeling of safety and survival relative to the world around us. When the stallion encounters the attempts of the caretaker to adjust their responses, there ensues a struggle for dominance between the caretaker and the stallion. This is most certainly a conscious undertaking on the part of the caretaker and a debatably unconscious attentiveness on the part of the stallion. Through repeated conditioning, the stallion comes to respond in the intended way established by the caretaker. The reinforcement can consist of either rewards, punishments or a combination of both. To persist in that reinforced training to the point where the behavior desired is observed and fairly stable arrives at a balance point between responsiveness and expressiveness that, essentially, allows the stallion's nature and character to remain relatively intact. There remains an expressiveness and individuality that is still characteristic to the individual stallion's nature. If the training is pursued well beyond the point of the shift into compliance, the stallion is pushed much further into submissiveness, thereby, slowly erasing or burying their innately individual character where it is replaced by the felt urgency for survival. At this point we can say that the stallion has been "broken' or, more specifically, we have "broken their spirit."

Each stallion's point of yielding is different. That point of yielding is his *Beta Point*. As long as the objective of the conditioning is reached before the *Beta Point* is reached, the stallion has the opportunity to negotiate a peaceful coalition between his ability to express his natural instincts and the level of conditioning required. At that point his character still has room to express itself and remains relatively intact. When the Beta Point is reached, too much reinforcement has been applied and the spirit is broken. When this occurs, the stallion's character is essentially extinguished.

Humans, as with stallions, are born into this world, with the shock of losing our safe and secure position in the womb to a loud and colder world and this is enough to push us into becoming more attentive to external circumstances. We are no longer as concerned with impulsiveness or expressiveness as we are at having to cope with the suddenly emerging discomfort of the new environment and circumstances that we, instinctively, sense as threatening our survival. However, even in the face of that struggle, there still remains a balance between our survival instincts and our capacity for individual expression. If there occurs a persistent and cumulative conditioning past the *Beta Point,* as with *toxic shame* or a traumatic event with enough intensity to invalidate the individual's sense of control by pushing past their *Beta Point*, the individual, essentially, gives up applying any effort at all in that area of his life affected if not all areas. In this circumstance we can say that the individual has learned how to be helpless. "Learned helplessness means a condition of a human person or an animal in which it has learned to behave helplessly, even when the opportunity is restored for it to help itself by avoiding an <u>unpleasant</u> or harmful circumstance to which it has been subjected. Learned helplessness theory is the view that <u>clinical depression</u> and related <u>mental illnesses</u> may result from a perceived absence of control over the outcome of a situation" (Wikipedia)(Seliman, 1975). As with the mechanism of depression, there is no longer the motivation to work toward their needs as there is now an expectancy of being invalidated or defeated with every effort. If we take this perception a bit further, we see the individual developing expectancy for being provided for by the world only on the "say so" of the conditioner, caretaker or people who are perceived as having a similar perspective. Internal motivation is no longer a factor except in conjointly exhibiting their need and helplessness to those they have chosen to believe have the control. This may evolve into the developing of many "luring" behaviors powered by a fearfulness and anxiety behind the voicing of their "request" emanating from their perceived ineffectualness and potential unworthiness. This scenario has been colorfully referred to as the "tyranny of the weak."

One last perspective that I feel needs to be added on the heels of depression, learned helplessness & trauma. That is one of self-sabotage. It is my belief that an individual who feels inferior, ineffectual and afraid of facing external influences that might negate their safe, familiar and diminished view of themselves is very likely liable to sabotage any circumstance that may threaten that security even though it would be perceived as a self improvement in the eyes of others. Their fear and belief is that they will have their perceived shame and inadequacy exposed through finding themselves totally out of control in the new frame. The applicable adage would be "keeping the devil you *do* know for fear of contending with the one that you *don't.*" Any action presenting a potential improvement that threatens their familiar diminished self image of inferiority and ineffectualness is quickly and unconsciously eradicated through creating circumstances that invalidate any potential self improvement or, conversely, promote self deprecation.

WHERE IS THE BALANCE?

Extreme *toxic shame* and pathological narcissism exist on extreme opposites of the range for sensitivity and insensitivity; *toxically shamed* individuals primarily being hyper-sensitive and *pathologically* narcissistic individuals primarily being hypo-sensitive. These two forces of direction exist in a polarity much the way yin and yang are represented in the I Ching. In perceiving the difference between black and white, we know that there are many grey areas between these two extremes. In this light we can say that as one changes into the other there is a point where black and white are equal in measure and represented by the most neutral grey where we cannot tell where one begins and the other ends. This is the point where there is a healthy amount of shame balanced with a healthy amount of narcissism. When these two qualities are in balance with each other, the emotions and sensitivities are settled and calm enough to allow the recognition and development of compassion. The subtlety of compassion requires that the heart be in a "quiet space." In this space, there is an absence of the need for defense mechanisms. In the same light, if we are balanced between *toxic shame* and narcissistic insensitivity we will also be in a state of balance between an external *locus of control* and an internal *locus of control* respectively. We can also say that there is a desirable balance between the qualities of acceptance and determinism, respectively.

WHAT HAPPENED TO COMPASSION?

At this point it may seem that I have digressed substantially from a discussion that might be related to compassion and you're probably wondering, "What has all this got to do with compassion?" The simplest answer would be that compassion is based on the *sharing* of feeling not the *polarizing* of it. Either extreme polarizes feelings and renders individuals unable to use or perceive compassion in its clearest form. Those who are motivated by mostly an external *locus of control* and host a feeling of *toxic shame* or *closet narcissism* are, essentially, preoccupied with a perceived lack in their self image and the need for its compensation. The number one concern is fear of exposure. This fear reinforces a polarity between themselves and what they fear. The number two concern is how to "make up" for the perceived lack in the self. For those who are motivated by a mostly internal *locus of control* and portray more of an *exhibitionist narcissism*; they are preoccupied with defending against "loss of face" by either walking away or unconsciously projecting their inadequacies on others through asserting themselves as superior. Their number one fear is the perceived loss of their control; which, consciously, they believe they have and unconsciously they know they don't.

Occupying either perspective to an extreme precludes an individual's ability to feel compassion as their attention is absorbed by their preoccupation with the perception of their own self-concept. How can they be aware of another's feelings if they are totally focused in how the self comes across to others? To feed into this polarity encourages competition; a further polarization.

COMPETITION & COMPARISON

To the social observer of our western culture, and many others, there is a very strong presence of competition underlying just about every activity that we undertake. We wish to "get ahead" financially. We wish to "come out on top" in relationships. We wish "our team" to win. We wish to get the best quality merchandise. We wish to have the best opportunity for advancement. We wish to "get there first." When "we win" we inch our way toward narcissism and a sense of superiority. When we "lose" we inch our way toward shame and the need for compensation for feeling inferior. We believe, or are told, that "everyone loves a winner" in spite of the fact that winning over others inspires, in them, envy, jealousy, resentment and a host of other rapport diminishing effects that polarize us against others. We are told that "no one wants to be a loser" in spite of the fact that we often see ourselves reflected in others who "don't come out on top" and push away from them so we don't feel the shame that we feel that *they* deserve. If we win too often we develop a mild case of ASN (*Acquired Situational Narcissism*). If we "lose" too often, we develop a mild case of depression with a need to primarily hide from the awareness of the failure or, to a lesser extent, compensate for our perceived inadequacies. Both outcomes push us further away from the balance point between *toxic shame* and narcissism. Compassion cannot survive in a state that includes the need for compensation or projection. Sometimes we are so obtuse to its meaning that we see ourselves in a race to see who is the most compassionate. This is truly an oxymoronic perspective. Yet, this is a perspective held by many people who have no understanding of what compassion truly is.

To claim to be compassionate when we are operating from a position of compensation for believed inadequacies or feigned superiority only serves to confirm our ulterior motives. How can we recognize another's pain or needs if our attention is focused on what we feel we are not or who we should be? We are preoccupied. We are "full" of ourselves. The feelings of our heart are blanketed. We are solidly rooted in the mind which assesses everything through comparison.

When we are being compassionate, we lean toward *intentionally empathizing* with the other person's feelings. If we are full of ourselves, we can't do that. If our heart isn't clear, the issues clouding it will obscure what we need to be sensitive to.

At this point you're saying to yourself, "But everyone has issues" and you'd be right. But there are issues and there are issues. Some issues are mostly surface and easy to work with. Others are extremely serious and emanate from a deeply subconscious root. Although we may not be willing to admit, we know how serious our issues are and understand that something must be done about them but, perhaps, are at a loss to understand *how* to handle them so they don't distort our humanitarian endeavors. In the upcoming sections I will attempt to offer alternative approaches to conventional psycho-therapeutic practices primarily focused on behavior modification; practices that only address the symptoms of a much deeper set of issues.

The MECHANISMS of the MIND

WHAT IS THE MIND?

Ask any person who they are and, invariably, they will tell you either their name or what they do. Both are labels. If they answer that they are an accountant, we immediately conjure an image of a desk with a computer, or if you're "old school," with many ledger books, very neatly arranged and containing many neat orderly rows of very small numbers. The person at the desk is very focused and wearing reading glasses. In their private life we would expect them to have a life and property composed of the bare essentials that are meticulously organized and in like new condition. Their car would be small, brown and well maintained. They are married with two and a half kids who are clean, neat, polite and well behaved. I think you've got a good grasp of the image that I'm painting. The point is, where does this image come from? It comes from our *past* experience and exposure to people we were told about by those we trust or those whom we have observed working as accountants. Our first encounter with an accountant may have produced an imprint of all these details but after that someone is introduced as an accountant and triggers a remembrance of that imprint, we will assume that the person possesses all the known qualities we've experienced even though they may be considerably different in their life and style of living.

The mind itself is nothing more than a biological computer gathering and labeling information for future encounters. It assesses, separates, judges and compares. For many people, however, they see themselves as *being* the mind. This should come as no surprise to us because we see our physical nature as a reflection of the mind through all its discriminations and comparisons. The mind, in its perception of the world, sees itself as a separate entity. This is the bottom line basis of our *ego*. It is that separateness or polarizing effect that enables us to determine our identity as individuated from the "outside" world. So then, to determine what we are, we must also determine what we are not. Our senses work in exactly the same fashion. To know what we are tasting, for example, we must compare it against what we *were* tasting *before* the experience. Therefore, the label we apply to "it" is solely dependent on the difference between the taste of "it" and what we last tasted before "it." Therefore, a memory or a stored prior imprint is a function of the separative mind and must also be considered as having occurred *before* "it." The other senses follow suit. In sight, we detect differences in the light. In hearing, we detect vibrational differences between previous and current sounds. In touch, we assess what we feel against what we have felt before. Since the mind can only operate within the context of polarity, it must also be considered one of the senses. This type of "thinking" is, in metaphysical terms, the *lower mind* and considered a function or quality that is circumscribed by the *solar plexus chakra*; an energy center or nerve ganglia located just below the sternum (this will be more deeply covered in a later section). The *lower mind's* field of operation exists within the constructs of logic and time. It handles the details of our movement through our physical world. At this point you are probably saying to yourself, "But my mind is much more than just the sorting of details" and you'd be right. The mind is actually composed of halves (again a polarity) and is fed by two different sources; the senses and intuition. The intuition, which I will also cover later in a discussion of the chakras, is a capacity that functions free from the constraints of time allowing a more subtle sensitivity to and comprehension of our abstract and conceptual perceptions. Even our intuition is not who we are but a tool we have at our disposal. More on that later. For now, let's just work with the *lower mind* and its operation within the constraints of time.

TIME, THE PAST, THE FUTURE & THE NOW

So much has been written about time, its meaning and implications for our perception of life as we know it. Yet, it's truly ironic how much we *don't* understand about time because we are so embroiled in the physical world. Trying to describe time in terms of the logic of the mind is much like trying to describe the color palette in terms of knowing only one color. If we are a fish living in the ocean, how can we describe land to another fish? Even if we have encountered it ourselves, it must be considered as a "peak" experience as described in the introduction of this book. To describe it, there must be a commonly grounded perception of land with the other fish we're describing it to; otherwise, there can be no transfer of comprehension.

The *ego* or the self exists in a linear temporality. That is, we perceive our existence within the confines of time which is linear. Let me explain. What we "know" today is based on what we experienced yesterday. What we will "know" tomorrow will be based on what we experience today. What we will know the day after tomorrow will be based on what we experience tomorrow. To this end, we can see that memory exists as a linear function through time. We must then ask what is time? In this frame we must say that it is the capacity of the mind to sequentially string together our experiences in an orderly fashion so we can use the order and information to predict what will come tomorrow and the day after. The sequential linearity of memories of our experiences is what gives us our perception of the self or *ego*. We then must go a step further and ask, "If there were no mind, would time still exist for us?" We can certainly say that if there were no mind, there would be no *ego*. The mind bases its "knowing" on what is now and what "came before" now. If there were no past, the mind would have nothing to compare against and, therefore, would have no perception of itself.

Right now you're probably scratching your head and saying what the devil is he talking about? How can I have no mind? Let's take this to a different slant. Those of you who have meditated know that when you are in your deepest and most peaceful meditation, the mind and its shenanigans are allowed to just drift past you without you giving them any consideration or attention. So, in this light, if the mind is just "free wheeling" and you're not involved, who is it that is being aware? However, the moment that you "stop" and ask that question, the mind kicks in and offers all sorts of explanations dependent on memories, past experiences and the feedback from other "fish" who have given you a static, defined position in their physical world. The peace you were just experiencing has just evaporated. Where did it go you ask? You're still within it but you've chosen to take a ride on the vehicle of the mind. You're the fish in the ocean who no longer perceives the ocean as anything different. You can feel the waves, the current, the temperature and the taste but you can no longer perceive the land it's encompassed by. You've just switched focus from the *higher mind* (free of time and powered by intuition) to the *lower mind* (defined by the constructs of time and powered by logic and comparison). You're back within the frame of the past, the present and future.

For those of you who have never meditated and have no idea what I'm talking about, I have a question for you. When was the last time you were totally involved in an activity; so much so that you lost track of time? You were so engrossed with, perhaps, painting a picture and five minutes later you looked at the time to see that *hours* have past since you began your activity. I'm sure it amazed you that you were in a space for so long and never realized you were "gone" to others in the physical world. When you're "in" the experience, you are experiencing timelessness or, what's been called, the eternal *now*. When you put your attention to defining it, you're no longer "having" the experience. The mind has taken over. *You are not your mind.* You *have* a mind; just like you *have* taste buds, you *have* ears, you *have* eyes and you *have* touch sensitivity. Your mind is, essentially, a sense organ and as such, it should be treated as one. What ever part of you is doing the perceiving through these tools is something timeless and completely different.

IN-TENTION

We all know that to have an intention is to propose an activity into which we will invest energy toward a future result. Whether we carry out this intention or not and why, then, adds a different focus. But suffice it to say, then, that since intention is directly relative to the time continuum, we can assume that to "have" or propose an intention is a function of the mind.

When we propose an intention, what are we actually doing? After much deliberation and going back and forth with the words used in the dictionary giving definitions for each other in an endless circle, I found that the word *tend*, which comes from the Latin word *tendere*, meaning to aim, stretch or reach outward, was the root word that needed meaning in order to give understanding to all the other words it gave rise to; intention, intense, detention, retention, attention, contend, pretend, extend and probably plenty more that I am at a loss to be aware of at the moment. The next question that begs to be answered is what is it that gets aimed or stretched and to where? The simplest answer is the application of our energy (focus). Let me explain. When something is stretched, as in a rubber band or a bow being pulled back before propelling an arrow, the force that creates the movement of the arrow or what holds items together in the rubber band is the application of our aimed energy (focus). In physics, we call this the ability to perform work. But what are we actually doing? The tension created between the two opposing forces is creating a polarity or *tension* that the universe seeks to return to an inert or balanced state through the application of *its* energy (focus). When the tension, polarity, energy or focus, is released or removed, the arrow is propelled and the items that were contained within the rubber band fall apart.

So, you might say, "Sure, that has to do with physics and the material world. But what has that got to do with my mind which I don't see as physical?" The fact is, just because we don't see evidence of our mind in the physical world doesn't mean that it doesn't apply or have an effect. Electricity operates just like the mind. We don't see it either, but, we certainly know that it has an effect. How? Let me use water as an example. And, yes, I know, water is physically tangible but, like all other mediums in the natural world, it operates under and responds to the same universal laws that govern electricity and the mind. For now, just accept the fact that the mind and electricity are the same in their behavior but just act in a less visible fashion than water.

Please imagine two containers. One contains water and the other is empty. Standing by themselves, it is likely that nothing will change except for a small amount of evaporation in the one filled with water over time. However, attach a small rubber tube at the base between them and a curious thing happens. The water in the full container drains just enough through the tube into the empty container to equalize the amount of water contained within each. The flow between them will continue until there is no more pressure or difference in their potential. The difference in potential is the fullness or push of water in the full container toward the empty container. They have, then, followed the laws of nature and have neutralized the difference in their potential. If we attach an open drain to the one that was originally empty and continually add a supply of water to the one that was full, the flow between will continue until we stop adding water and both containers have emptied. By adding the drain and the supply, what we have done is maintained a difference in pressure or potential between the two containers creating a flow of water through the natural action of the universe attempting to neutralize the difference. Following the same laws and in a much larger scope, this is the natural action of the evolving universe attempting to reunite all parts of itself. In another light we might also say that this energy is equivalent to the power of love attempting to reunite us all. Electricity operates the same way. The two containers, or poles, are maintained at a difference in potential. When we add wiring between the two poles, much like adding a tube between the two containers, it's like turning on the power switch allowing the two poles to flow between each other attempting to eliminate the difference in potential according to universal law. The end, where the drain would be, is the place where we would apply the energy to do work and the other end, where the full container is refilled, we would consider our power supply. Remove the tube or the wiring and the work stops.

Let's now return to our concern with *intention*. Since the mechanism of the mind is to separate, every time we label something we separate ourselves from it and create a difference in potential between ourselves and what we label. We now perceive what we labeled as being "outside" of ourselves. Let's take this one step further. When we "set" an intention, we identify a goal by separating ourselves from it. Essentially, much like a syringe creating a vacuum to pull fluid into the chamber, we create an empty space in our minds expecting the universe to fill it with what we think we are in need of. Intention, ambition and desire all fall under the same bailiwick; focusing on a perceived lack with the hope or expectation of it being filled by the universe much like the empty container is filled by the full one.

Now that we have all the hypothetical understandings in place, let's set up an analogy. The endless source of energy that the universe provides for us is the water that continually refills the container. Our participation in the world is where the draining of the container empties the water to. Our mind is what separates one container into two requiring us to insert a tube between them in order to continue the flow. Our belief and trust in the world and ourselves is the act of applying a tube between the containers and a wire between the poles. If we choose to believe that we *cannot* have or accomplish what we have set ourselves apart from, no tube or wire is inserted and we remain stagnant with no flow of energy. The universe has no need to rebalance itself. If we chose to believe that we *can* have or accomplish what we have set ourselves apart from, a tube or wire is inserted and we provide a path allowing the universe to rebalance itself giving us what we desire.

Let's recap our premises. When we "set" an intention, we are creating an *inner polarity* or difference of potential *within ourselves* (the two containers or poles) which is then capable of performing action or work provided we provide a path for them to neutralize by way of our beliefs. If we look at the word *intention*, it comes from *in-* and *-tendere*; *-tendere* is the process of aiming and *in-* is, literally, pointing inward. Coupled with this we must remember that the mind separates or creates a difference where the universe attempts to reunite the opposing forces that we have separated. A *desire* can be compared to a polarity in that it is the mind that creates a separation between what we believe (think) we don't have in our need to feel complete or unified (the basic state of the universe). So intentions, ambitions and desires are "siblings" in a family of perceived need within our "mind space."

The most important principle to be understood here is that if we don't believe that we can, we will block our own ambitions, desires and intentions through not building the bridge required by the universe in order to allow its flow through us.

THE ISSUE OF PURPOSE

In looking at intention, we must also consider purpose. Our most common understanding of purpose is that it is something that was previously intended. The word purpose originates from the 13th century Old French word *porpos* meaning "aim or intention" and from the root *pose* in 14th century French meaning to "put in a certain position." It is also related to the Late Latin word *pausare* meaning "to halt, rest or pause." If we roughly interpolate the meaning, we can say that purpose is to "aim at halting or pausing." From this we can assume that it's aiming toward the completion of something.

You might say that I'm splitting hairs and you'd, probably, be right. Their meanings are so close as to blur the veracity of what appears to make them seem different. The way I would interpret this difference is that to have an intention is to *aim* at taking a particular *action*. The *result* of the action might be important but the word intention, more appropriately, refers to the movement toward the *act* itself. The word purpose, especially in our present day culture, relates to something in need of completion or ending. We see a purpose as the *object* of our intention "requesting" or needing our action. Remember, to objectify something is a function of the mind where it separates the observer from the observed. Think back to the two containers of water. The pressure of the full container enables the intention and the empty container enables the purpose or perceived need. In other words, the fullness of the container can be seen as having the "motivation" or "urge" to move the water and the empty container has a "need" of its *movement* toward being filled representing the perfect Yin / Yang relationship.

It's important to remember that it is the mind that has divided the one container into two thereby requiring a reconnection allowing the flow back toward unity. The mind is acting within its parameters by acting and reacting between the polarities that condition all physical life. If the mind did not separate intention from purpose through the mechanism of time, they would still be the same energy. There would be no before, after or now requiring a reunion.

Let's take our division one step further. If we see our lives in terms of purpose, we see it in terms of something needing to be completed. By subjecting ourselves to the something needing to be completed, we are responding to an external *locus of control*. If we see our lives in terms of setting intentions, we see our lives as a function of the internal urges we feel and are responding to an internal *locus of control*. If we are equally balanced between internal and external *loci of control*, there exists no difference between purpose and intention. We perceive them both as the same energy. We, then appear to be balanced and living in the eternal "now."

The most important point to understand is that intention and purpose are both functions of the mind and can only exist in a reality where time is functioning. In this light, the idea of an eternal God having a purpose or plan for us seems pointless. In accepting that there *is* a God and that he *is* eternal, there is no time for purpose and intention to function within. Intelligent design, as well as "having a plan for us" then becomes a mute point.

At this point, I'm sure that there are many of you feeling that I've insulted your beliefs. The word now needing clarification and understanding is *belief*. Let's move on.

BELIEF IS A CHOICE, FAITH IS...SOMETHING ELSE

In our modern times, if you ask someone what their beliefs are, you'll get a wide range of descriptions from religion to science and all the variations in between. Originally, there were only seven major religions and any variations in life styles were inevitably connected to one of those religions. Since the early 60s we've exponentially expanded our awareness of the number of variations that a belief can be expressed in way beyond the few life styles and religions that were common throughout the preceding seven hundred years. Yet, the past fifty years have become diversified more than any other period in our history.

Much like intention and purpose, belief and faith are interactive in a similar way. What's puzzling is the "flip" in their manner of use that took place early on. In the early thirteenth century the word *belief* was primarily used in reference to our trust in a deity and *faith* was used in relating to loyalty to a *person* based on an agreed upon or implied promise or duty. In the fourteenth century a curious thing happened. Their applied use flipped. *Faith*, a cognate of the Latin word *fides* took on a religious implication and *belief* became restricted to the "mental acceptance of something as true." Also, from the thirteenth century, the Latin word *convenier,* meaning to agree or to meet, has become paired with our current day interpretation of *faith* and is now inextricably interwoven with the word *covenant* meaning a pact with a deity. This left the word *belief* as a conjugate of meanings relating to facts, proof and evidence which took hold more strongly with the advents of the Protestant Reformation, Martin Luther, the beginnings of the Age of Reason and the development of the scientific method. The most appropriate point in time culminating what we might call a historical beginning for these forces occurred when Martin Luther posted what is commonly know as the "95 Thesis," protesting the sale of church indulgences, on the door of the Castle Church of Wittenberg on All Saints Day, October 31, 1517AD.

So, when we say we believe something, what are we saying? We're saying that we accept a proposed or encountered paradigm or pattern of thinking as having validity or at least an agreed upon acceptance by others as being "true." So, for example, to accept that gravity is a "fact" we have "evidence" through observing its dynamics and through being informed by others as to its validity, whether through word of mouth or publications. So, essentially, as humans there are two ways in which we can judge something spoken or written as having validity for us; either through our own direct experience or from a source that we "trust." The word *trust* dates back to the thirteenth century Old Norse word *traust* meaning confidence. We can see that *con-* relates to bringing together and –*fidence* comes from *fides* meaning *belief*. This brings us back where we started. However, the Gothic word *trausti* relates to agreement. So, having a source that we *trust* is simply saying that we agree with and accept as valid the information that we have received from them. If we accepted their "hear say" as valid, we would most likely have had prior dealings with them and judged valid what they presented to us because we had judged their beliefs as matching *our* perception of our reality. We then would be depending on the validity of *their* experiencing as long as we continued to *trust* their judgment.

The other words that come up when we are dealing with validity are *facts*, *evidence* and *proof*. *Fact* comes from the Latin word *factum* from the 1530s meaning event or occurrence. This relates to our experience. *Evidence* comes from the fourteenth century Latin word *evidentia* meaning proof. *Proof* comes from the early thirteenth century Old French word *preove* meaning "evidence to establish the fact of something." So you see, we go round and round with our meanings. In the final analysis, it is *we* who must accept the validity of whatever we *choose* to include in our personal paradigm. A *belief* is not something that happens to us. It is chosen.

OBJECTIVE and SUBJECTIVE

For those who base their perception of reality mostly on what their physical senses (the mind included) report to them, the word *objective* is of tremendous importance. Their definition of self comes from the reflection that their perceived sense of the world delivers to them. Hence, they define themselves on what lies "outside" of the self or how they perceive the world *reacting* to them. In itself, this relates to a determined exterior *locus of control*. Since there is a separation of self and "outside" the self, we can assume that the most important operating sense is the mind. The other five senses merely confirm or deny what the mind has postulated about our world. The senses, in and of themselves, make no judgment or separation.

For those who base their perception of reality mostly on what they feel (an uncontrolled movement *within* themselves), the word *subjective* is of tremendous importance. Their definition of self comes from the feeling produced by their own generation of movement in the world. Hence, they define themselves on what lies "inside" the self or how they perceive their *actions* on the world. In itself, this relates to an interior *locus of control* orientation.

Please remember that there will be times in which we are externally motivated and other times where we are internally motivated. We are a mix of both. The more the ratio between them differs, the more easily we will be perceived as being more of one than the other.

The concurrent understanding for this is that the externally activated person (primarily reactive) will perceive reality as being *static* through being defined by facts and external occurrences even though those circumstances, in reality, are dynamic. The mind, essentially, takes "snapshots" of the world in order to solidify circumstances for its assessment. They will say that all reality is *objective*. The internally activated person (primarily proactive) will perceive reality as being *dynamic* through being defined by the ever changing movement of their feelings and internal "occurrences." They will say that all reality is *subjective*. Depending on where the initiation of our perception emanates from will have everything to do with how we view reality.

It is also very likely that we will see life as being regulated objectively in some circumstance and subjectively in others. For example, someone may see themselves as being at the mercy of circumstances surrounding their job but feel that they are "in control" of their relationships. This may seem perfectly fine to the individual having the perception but an onlooker may perceive cognitive dissonance in that individual's approach since career and relationships issues could be viewed as being interdependent. Remember, separation occurs in the mind and our belief about who "controls" what situations is purely an individual choice. In the overall scheme of things, *all reality must be subjective* since it must first be perceived and accepted as having validity for us. If you're not "there" to perceive it or don't hear validation from a source you trust, it doesn't exist for you. It goes way back to the question: If a tree falls in the forest, does it make a sound?

METAPHYSICAL & META-PSYCHOLOGICAL CONSIDERATIONS

YOUR POINT of REFERENCE

Thus far I have talked about worldly perceptions, empathy, levels of awareness, scientific, psychological and philosophical approaches. I have used these paradigms to set the stage for a broader and much more subtle framework to approach compassion with by using the dynamics of energy. However, the subject of human energy, the chakras and their existence, let alone their effects, currently endures an extremely slow and resistant acceptance by the proponents of the scientific method who are so deeply rooted in the tangible world. Yet, one can only wonder that with such a rich history of experience and documentation in the ancient world of so many cultures why such a resistance still endures. Tangibility is the preferred medium of the discriminating mind. But, as I have alluded to in the past pages, all action emanates from something more than just the mind. The judgment and the categorization that the mind performs is an after effect or residue of something else that has proceeded it. The movement of our feelings and the "surfacing" of our thoughts come from deeper and more subtle origins. To put it into words limits us to a level of perception that the mind is able to discriminate. It's a lot like telling a blind man what light is. Even though the blind man is surrounded by light, he is unable to experience it as a sighted person might. This goes back to our fish in the ocean being unable to perceive the water as a separate quality until it is able to experience the land that surrounds it enough to "see" or perceive a difference. Another way to understand this, especially for those of you with a scientific temperament, would be to compare this to the workings of an electromagnet. It's easy to see and feel its tangible qualities; the metal, the wiring, but to perceive the field that surrounds and permeates it; you must first realize that it is there and then you must have a tool and some reference to measure it against. Those of us who use our feeling as our gauge for reality will find it much easier to accept this "intangible" dimension than someone who uses their mind as their template for reality. Nevertheless, the tree falling in the forest *does* make a sound but only for whomever else is listening. For those of you who are feeling oriented, you know where I'm going. For those of you, who are of the scientific orientation, please, if you can, withhold judgment until you have heard me out. The framework I will describe is solid and cohesive but extremely difficult to measure without tools specific to this kind of energy. Perhaps, future scientific methods will develop measuring tools sensitive to the domains I will describe.

CHAKRAS & AWARENESS

In the same fashion that we have nerve plexus' conjoining at various areas in the body, we also have energy plexus' that overlay those junctures. In metaphysical traditions these areas are called *chakras*. The word *chakra* comes from the Sanskrit meaning wheel. Hence, the points in the body where the *chakras* are positioned are also called vortexes. Since sound, light and energy travels in cycles, these serve as good examples for how energy moves in the *chakras*; also spinning in cycles. The faster they spin, the higher the frequency. The slower they spin, the lower the frequency. In the same way that it can be determined which way the energy will flow through an electromagnet (by changing the polarity); we also have the capability to determine the direction the energy will flow cycling in the chakra (projecting or receiving). Suffice it to say for now that if the spin, from our vantage point, is counterclockwise, the energy will be moving toward you. If moving clockwise, away from you. Hence we can say it is moving inward or outward. For example, to take this concept further; when we are speaking, the energy will flow clockwise and away from us (outward). When we are listening, the energy will be flowing counterclockwise and toward us (inward).

The chakras are "connected" to many different references, qualities and aspects of all life. These correspondences are endless since they permeate and include every aspect of human existence. To delineate them here would be a monumental task that can be covered better by the multitude of books currently on the market. My aim here is to describe the "head space" and cognitive perception of an individual who "operates" on each of the levels. To this end I will endeavor to build an awareness of an individual's perspectives by referring back to the "Sequential Progression of Awareness" chart covered previously.

Before covering each level, it's important to understand the building effect of moving from one center to the next. To do so requires us to move through them *sequentially*. That is, we cannot "skip" one center to move to the next. What is contained in each center must necessarily be ingested and integrated in order to comprehend and use what is being offered through the next center. In a sense, we can call this a chain of command. To skip the experience needed to develop the capacity inherent to the next sequential level in order to "move up the ranks" leaves us at a deficit for what must be understood before we can apply our skills effectively. In business, this is called the "Peter Principle" where an individual is promoted beyond his capabilities. In a grosser comparison, might say that one who crawls needs to learn to walk before they can run.

Additionally, when I describe "where" the *chakra* or center is located in the body, I will give the location to which it has traditionally been applied but we must realize that when a center is actively assimilated and integrated, that area will extend outward. How far it extends or, more appropriately, how intensely the field may be developed depends on the maturity and awareness of the person the field emanates from. Its emanation is a function of both the projective and receptive capacities of the individual. So a person who has only recently begun to work with the center may only appear to resonate within a mere point in the body, where a person who has integrated the qualities may "broadcast" well past the borders of his body. We should also realize that though a person may have assimilated and integrated the energies of that center, it is not a permanent condition and that the individual may easily regress toward a prior more limiting perspective of life based on grosser desires and the gained abilities may go dormant until the perceptive state is again achieved. The only difference between one who has lost capacity and one who has just gained is the ease and speed with which that center is then again resonated with. Understand that when I say resonated with, I am referring to returning at a state of perception more broadly centered than the center the individual has recently "graduated" from.

The Root Center

The root center, or *Muladhara* in Sanskrit, is located at the entry point of the vagina on a female and the position of the prostate on the male. This is both where the individual's life energy enters from the bottom part of the bodily trunk and where a reservoir of energy called the *kundalini* resides that is the starting point for the circulation or flow of energy up through the other chakras. The other "polarity" of life energy enters through the crown chakra which will be covered later.

This center is solely focused in relieving the stress or polarity created by the necessities of survival. To this end it is mobilized toward the acquisition of food, shelter and perpetuation of the species. It is an almost tangible mix of mind and instinct in which there is little awareness of anything other than the lack of survival needs that prevent the reduction of the insecurity associated with the absence of feeling comfortable and sated. The objective, essentially, is to recreate the conditions that were present before the individual exited from the womb. In this "headspace" there is only a selfish orientation directed toward its own comfort and pleasure. We could say that this might be a parallel focus to that of Freud's *id*. Any sense of awareness indicative of empathy or compassion will be completely absent. The only awareness present is the feeling of separation from whatever it is that will neutralize felt or imagined desires. This center may also be compared to the physiological needs corresponding to the first level of "Maslow's Hierarchy of Needs:" breathing, food, water, sex, homeostasis and excretion (Maslow, 1943). Any sexual activity will be almost totally directed toward achieving orgasm. Any partner will suffice. The qualities of the partner are unimportant except for their capacity to enable the facilitation the orgasm. By itself, the physical orgasm is an almost total but temporary reduction of physical tension. The urge is driven by the natural polarity developed by the "separation of the sexes." The physical bond that is created might be considered "future insurance" for the satisfying of their desires, yet, a future awareness is not present.

In terms of human feeling, our comfort within our own body is also a function of the root center. Those who have a "disconnect" or a discomfort with they way they feel within their own body will have difficulties in creating physical relations with members of the opposite sex. Those who appear to possess an "animal magnetism" are generally more comfortable with their own sexuality thereby producing a much larger component of sex hormones than those who have been "unsuccessful" in the acquisitions of partners. Indiscriminant choice for sexual activity is, usually, an indication of an individual operating from a root center orientation. Root center activity operates almost exclusively in the moment. There is, essentially, no planning or regard, let alone awareness, for consequences. The actions are totally reactive. Adrenaline and the "fight or flight" instinct are also connected to the root center.

The Sacral Center

The sacral center, or the *Swadhisthana* in Sanskrit, is located three inches below the belly button in a line with the "small" of the back. The center itself is inside the body but just in front of the spine. This center is primarily concerned with balance. In the martial arts it is also known as the *Tan Tien* center (pronounced *dan cheeyen*). Physically, it is the center point of gravity for the entire body. It is also the storage point for *chi* or life energy and considered the lower part of the *triple warmer* as related to martial art practices.

This chakra is considered to be equivalent to a "tribal" orientation (Ruumet, 2006). In terms of Maslow's needs, it fulfills the level of belonging and relational bonding. It is held from the perspective of what the individual may gain from any group or relationship they choose to be part of. It is mostly selfish and is part of the survival mindset but from less than a physical orientation. It is believed that emotional security and well being can be gained through bonding with others who may have "an edge" or a capacity that might contribute to that end. We might say that it exemplifies "safety in numbers."

This level of awareness works with reciprocal giving and receiving. Focus on another person is more in terms of them being a vehicle to and end rather than as an individual. In this light most people are viewed "en masse." The only differences might be when one individual or group has a specific possession or quality that would be seen as, again, giving "an edge" to the purveyor. There is a rudimentary form of awareness receptive of empathy but only in terms of what is needed or wanted by the empathizer and how it will affect their survival and comfort "status."

Sex on this level is in terms of catharsis relative to specific needs, taste and tension. The individual who best fits those tastes and qualities with the ability to relieve specific types of tension would be sought out and potentially retained for future release. In this way, the individual would feel possessive of the person(s) with these qualities with the idea of them potentially sating their specific needs in the future. More evolved relationships may be possible but only as an "accidental" result of their pursuits.

Any group possessing preferred specific qualities would be sought after and joined for the benefits. These would include conventional religion, unions, politics or any other groups focused on their combined social usefulness for the purpose of having the pick of individuals with preferred or needed qualities from a "larger gene pool."

The person "stranded" here by retarded emotional development would be seen as being poorly socialized.

The Solar Plexus

The solar plexus center, or the *Manipura* in Sanskrit, is located in a line from the notch underneath the bottom of the sternum to the middle of the back just in front of the spine. It is the center of nourishment in all senses of the word. First, it is a major food processing point and the place where we "digest" the feelings we perceive relative to others. It is, also, the emotional center of the body where we register our "gut feeling." In the same way we register whether we are hungry relative to our stomach being full or not, it also is where we decide whether our individual need for recognition by others is filled or not.

In Maslow's Hierarchy of Needs, this level corresponds to that of esteem but can be separated into two levels. The lower level corresponds to status, recognition, prestige or fame as received from or applied by others. Its *locus of control* is predominantly external. The higher level relates to how one relates to one's self. That is, do we have self respect, confidence or strength as acquired from personal experience? Its *locus of control* is predominantly internal. Both levels operate within the realm of the solar plexus but the higher level is closer to acquiring the perspective of operating from the heart center in that its *locus of control* is more internal through, essentially, being less focused on the opinions of others.

Here, the concept of an *inferiority complex* (Adler, 1927), as outlined by Alfred Adler, finds fertile ground when acknowledgment from others is not acquired when operating on the lower level. It may also be manifested on the higher level but not with the intensity that it might be felt on the lower level due to inadequacy reinforcements perceived to be coming from external sources. It is, also, here that learned helplessness will take a dominant foothold.

In the same vein, it is the seat of the "lower mind" (separative in nature) where we acknowledge the individuality of others and compare ourselves to those whom we have acknowledged. This center is also considered to be equivalent with our "need to be special" (Ruumet, 2006). In this light, it is the major center in which we will feel the quality of pride and, of course, shame; toxic or not. Hence, our need for compensation emanates here geared toward gaining a sense of "feeling full." Taken one step further, this will also be a major center dealing with addictions of all kinds.

Both feelings and emotions are registered and dealt with here. It is very important at this point to make a distinction between them.

Feeling is a wave that moves through the body, generally, without our volition. Yet, our body is much more than just its physical constituents. In the same fashion that we emanate an electromagnetic field as explained in a previous section on empathy, that field also, to some extent and depending on our sensitivity, may extend past the boundary of our physical body. Through the vehicle of that field we are able to perceive variations in other energy fields meeting ours much like a fish would sense a change in the water currents surrounding it as another fish swims past. Call it our "seventh sense" (as the sixth is actually the mind). We can compare it in human terms to where we are in a room and someone enters quietly enough to where our physical senses register no sound, sight or scent indicating their presence but "something else" tells us that they are there. Their electromagnetic field came close enough and pressed against ours enough to where we felt a difference in the "feel" of our surrounding environment. The more tranquil we and the environment are, the wider our "range" of awareness would have relative to their entrance. As love, anger, sadness, joy and other feelings are perceived by us, they also radiate out and around us through our electromagnetic field. As another person approaches us radiating *their* feelings, we not only receive a "proximity alert" but our awareness is also colored by the *type* of feeling that the other person is radiating. As their field contacts ours in the same way that two balloons might "bump" into each other, our familiarity with the type or "color" of the field they radiate triggers a resonant chord within us resurfacing the experiences in which we became familiar with the same type of feeling. With the resonant trigger resurfaces all the judgments, thoughts, memories and beliefs that we hold relative to our previous experiencing of that feeling. At this point, feeling becomes transformed into emotion. Feelings only occur *in the moment* while we are experiencing them. The moment that the mind becomes involved, they become emotions. The word emotion comes from 12th century Latin meaning to move out or agitate; *ex-*, out + *movere*, to move. The moving out is, essentially, our separating from directly experiencing the feelings to becoming an observer and describer of them. Being separated from them through analysis and through labeling, we are no longer experiencing the feelings "first hand." Most of the time and in most people, the act of resonating, generally, activates this separative thought process that occurred when we first felt the feelings and shifted to analyzing them. However, there are times when this does *not* occur as in when we are either dancing or having sex with someone so intensely that we are totally consumed by the feelings the experience generates. Waves of energy wash over the body. The feeling of union, or reunion for the metaphysically oriented, is overwhelmingly pleasurable. It is only when we step back and start to think about the experience that the feeling morphs into emotion. The quality of union or reunion that takes place in dancing and sex is more a function of the heart center where we lose our sense of self in the experience.

There are occasions where the intensity of the immediate experience is *so* strong that the *egoic* propensities of the mind are not strong enough to break through our absorption enough to allow it the ability to regain its usual control over our life force. Our culture's extreme preoccupation with the physical world and its standing demand for all manner of reality to be "evidence" based has left us all convinced that the "lower mind" is indeed *supposed* to be in control in all of our life dealings. We must remember that to have "evidence" is to simply have an agreement for and acceptance of the hypothesized truth of a belief by a large number of people. Historically, a large number of people also agreed that the earth was flat. Need I say more?

The physical senses are portals to triggering feeling and emotion but are not necessarily the only avenue. As we resurface the memory of a past experience, we also may trigger the initial feeling perceived when we first had the experience. But, like the original experience that the memory resurfaced, it quickly becomes relegated to the machinery of the mind and morphed into an emotion(s).

It is important to note that it is in this center that the majority of our population resides in. Since the solar plexus is the home of the "lower mind," it is also the seat of possessiveness, especially, relating to things that we have strong feelings and emotions concerning. Most of our population is extremely possessive though our acknowledged ideal for social expectation demands the *expression* of an "ethically higher" behavior while silently ignoring the more selfish emotions that are tacitly *suppressed* let alone acknowledged or expressed. There is a tacit and colluded underlying attitude held by the "silent majority" that suppresses any human characteristics exposing our selfish animal nature as expressed by the id. Winning, acquiring and becoming are personal enhancements which should be striven for, yet, downplayed according to these standards. Pride should be *felt* but not *displayed* unless it is for someone other than the self. This becomes quite apparent when we see bumper stickers proclaiming that "My child is an honors student at Robot Elementary." Any sense of competitiveness is internally striven for but externally denied. Some of the only places where open competition and display for recognition is "allowed" or tolerated is in sports and part of the corporate sector. In these areas yielding is unacceptable and seen as a weakness. Generally, the word "allowing" is not a word used relative to the solar plexus except in the capacity of the one who receives.

The Heart Center

The heart center, or *Anahata* in Sanskrit, lies in a line from dead center of the sternum to a point 3" below where the neck meets the shoulders in front of the spine. It is the center of giving and releasing in all senses of the word. In the same way that the solar plexus emphasizes a perspective focused on acquisition and possessiveness, this center embodies the opposite perspective focused on selflessness and giving. It embodies the highest values of what the compassionate portion of our culture strives to emulate and project, but please note that there is an ongoing battle with the naturally selfish instinct and perspective "residing" in the solar plexus which is still acquisitive and possessive in its orientation. We are still animals and responsive to our senses, yet, due to our evolving nature we occasionally find ourselves in the heart center mind set of giving. Whether this is at the desired "higher focus" encouraged by those who operate from this center or from the direct experiential enlightenment of those who attain that preponderant perspective, it is, nevertheless, still a quality of yielding, giving, releasing, "letting go" or any attitude that lightens our personal connection to the material world.

As perceived through sex, this center's intensity of experience can range from blissful sharing all the way to the point of fierce abandon. The quality of selflessness allows for total openness in the experience. In it is a "loss of self."

In "letting go" there is a word of caution needed. This quality can also be used as a vehicle for escaping or avoiding one's responsibility for themselves. An individual may "let go" of much more than what is prudent for remaining a "responsible" adult. Additionally, those who espouse to "let go and let god" may also be shirking the necessary effort required for handling their own difficulties. In this light absolution can certainly be viewed by some as a convenient escape.

In light of the fact that the center before, the solar plexus, is self oriented, this "letting go" may also be seen in the light of looking for something greater than the self in spite of the fact that the initial motivation emanates from our natural *instinct* to search for advantage. This encouraged searching is also a fledgling product of our curiosity and urge to know. In Maslow's Hierarchy of Needs (Maslow, 1943) he describes this level as indicative of aesthetic needs and our desire to understand. The word *aesthetic* comes from the Greek *aisthanesthai* "to perceive (by the senses or by the mind), to feel." The word *understanding* leads us to the 14th century Latin word *comprehendere* from *com-* "completely" + *prehendere* "to catch hold of, seize, unite." The implication is that we are seeking some sort of unity or common thread that connects us to a larger "meaning," direction or purpose. This has given rise to aestheticism which has become an avenue for self exploration and meaning through art, music and activities imitating life in a way that we are able to see the common threads of our humanity. Beauty, after all, is our wonder in seeing the perfection of form as related to the matrix of our perceived reality.

This center is also considered to be equivalent of the "disappearance of difference" (Ruumet, 2006). In that light we can say that it is the center where competition, comparison, elitism and specialness are absent and that humility is encouraged for any person feeling idealized by others through being imbued with any "special" quality. Additionally, contemporary New Age spirituality suggests the "emptying" of oneself in order that the universe may fill the individual with what is *needed* for the evolution of the masses. Naturally, those who appear to be *in need* become the ready vessels for focused releasing and the vehicle for the individual's anticipated enlightenment. Under these circumstances the perceived meaning of a *need* and its definition requires clarification along with its confusion and overlap with the meanings of *wants* and *desires*.

To look at the word *need* and *necessity*, one would assume that their meanings come from the same root. However, they don't. *Need* comes from the 12th century Saxon word *nied* meaning "a necessity, compulsion or a duty." The word necessity comes from the 14th century Latin word *necessarius*, composed of *ne-* "not" + *-cedere* meaning "to withdraw, go away." To be unnecessary then translates to a desire (12th century Old French *desirrer* "wish, desire, long for") and a want (11th century Old Norse vanta, "to be lacking"). **The indespensible part seems to be mostly attached to a *need*.** In this light I perceive the words *need* and *necessity* relating to the survival of the individual. I then see a *desire* or a *want* as the product of a real or imagined lack. They can be *necessary* or not, but that determination is specific to the individual's own experience. This may seem like splitting hairs but the meanings of the words in our contemporary vernacular have become so distorted by time and differing influences that it has lead to radically different assumptions about their meanings. How words are interpreted depends on the varied history of who you speak with. Let's move on to their application.

To neither *want* nor *need* anything from others we are essentially incoercible by them and, barring any external circumstances, are free to choose our life path of action to the fullest extent possible. For us to be susceptible to coercion designed by others there must be a *need* or *want* that others can use as a bargaining point for their coercion. To begin to understand the dynamics, let's look at the difference between a *need* and a *want*.

A *need* is a requirement or something that we believe that we cannot do without. A *want* is described as a wish or a preference. A *need* would then hold much more potential for the individual wishing to manipulate someone. Generally accepted among *needs* are air, water, food and shelter. The result of the absence of air and water are easily understandable. These are things without which we will eventually die. However, there is, for example, a very large difference between eating raw vegetables or veal cordon bleu and living in a cave or a million dollar mansion. All these things can nourish and protect us but do so in varying degrees. The "style of life" that we are accustomed to usually determines how we differ in what we consider to be a *want* or a *need*. For example, someone who has never done without the million dollar mansion or veal cordon bleu would swear that they *need* these things for their survival. Yet, after going without these things and being forced to live in a cave on raw vegetables, they would come to realize that they *need* less than they thought they did because they have never lived through the challenge of doing so previously. They may now *want* or prefer these things but know that they are not necessary or required for their survival. In this way we can say that challenge is a catalyst for developing self confidence and self sufficiency. For most people, this is a common dynamic. Conversely, the person who has lived in a cave and eaten raw vegetables all their lives would never miss the mansion or the veal cordon bleu and would realize, after having them, that they might be pleasurable but that they really didn't *need* them for their survival. They might also look at the person who thought they were *needs* with puzzlement.

So, the difference between *need* and *want* is generally the product of an individual's perception, experience and how it is applied. This is true of both the one having the *need* or the *want* and the observer. The heart often misinterprets this difference simply due to the fact that they may have had little or no experience or understanding concerning the history of the individual appearing to have what they perceive as a *need*. The heart center individual is an easy target for those who are accustomed to coercing others to provide what they profess to *need* but in reality only *want*, so as not to have to exert any effort in attaining it. Others may really believe that they have a *need* or they may *consciously* coerce heart center individuals into becoming their providers even if they are fully capable of providing for themselves. In either case, the heart center individual often becomes the "gift that keeps on giving" unless they still retain a strong component of the solar plexus perspective or have an "understanding" that the throat center provides.

An important aspect of the seven chakra center matrix is that everyone has the potential to operate from all the centers in varying combinations and at varying times in there lives but that there is always a perspective that the individual is most consistent in thereby indicating which center the individual's perspective on life primarily "resides." While the centers operate in conjunction with each other, the individual's immediate circumstance, assimilated experience and current outlook usually determines which one is dominant at any particular time. The most common combinations are those of any two centers "next" to each other indicating a potential position of growth for that individual. For example, if the individual is struggling with inclinations of being either giving or possessive, their current point of developing would reside between the heart center and solar plexus center. Generally, one center would be dominant depending on any given situation but the individual would oscillate between the two perspectives until one set of values or understandings gained a dominant foot hold empowering one center over the other. The laws of energy dictate that empowerment is accomplished by the consistent focusing of our attention. Energy always follows attention. So, whichever quality was most focused on would eventually become the dominant influence. Additionally, regressing from one center "down" to another may just as easily occur as moving "up," especially, if the external pressure to do so is more powerful than their dedication to their "values" of the higher center. In this case, *locus of control* plays an extremely important part in terms of how they will respond to external influences.

It should also be noted that motivation toward action is much less visible to those operating from the "lower" or "materially oriented" centers. Those are the centers located below the heart center. Someone operating from the solar plexus center would have no understanding as to why the heart center person does what they do, especially, if their action was dictated by the throat center or higher. With the heart center being imbued with a lighter and more subtle capacity for awareness, the heart center person would have a broader perspective in their understanding of others due to the inclusive nature of selflessness, whereas, the solar plexus person would only see others as a reflection of their own needs and possessiveness. To a solar plexus center person, someone operating from the heart center may be seen as weak and impotent due to the yielding nature of the heart center and they would never understand why the heart center person didn't "take" what they needed. To the solar plexus center person, any person that is internally focused or that does not appear to create external action toward their own advantage would be interpreted as having inherent weakness. However, just because someone doesn't create external action from an internal motivation, we must not assume that they are directed by an internal *locus of control.*

The breadth of perspective for each center is separated by their ability to distinguish between different levels of subtle difference. One of the ways of exemplifying the differing subtleties between the centers is to look at the different states of water. An ice cube has a limited range in terms of movement and perspective. Whatever shape it is in is the only perspective that is available to it. Water in its liquid state is much more adaptable and can morph itself into different perspectives *surrounding* the ice cube from all sides and having three hundred and sixty degrees worth of vantage points. Water vapor has the variability of both but also possesses the ability to also *permeate* the other two adding another dimension. When we move from ice to liquid and then to gas, it is a similar change as we move from one center to the next in an ascending direction. Each center yields an extra dimension allowing a broader perspective than the one preceding it.

So, at this point we can say that the heart center, devoid of all other influences (if that is possible) is totally receptive, yielding, selfless and giving. It is mindless. Any action taken in its interest will be directed by either the solar plexus or the throat center. It will also be important to know that the heart center is the pivotal point between the upper and the lower centers.

The Throat Center

The throat center, or *Vishuddha* in Sanskrit, lies in a line between a spot just above the larynx and back from the chin to the hollow in the base of the skull. This center is generally referred to as the center of will. This is the place on the throat were we develop a "lump" when we have something to assert but have difficulty saying it. This is a more contemporary connection to our aspect of will. One of the earliest uses of the word *will* comes from the 4 century B.C. Sanskrit *vrnoti* and Gothic *waljan* meaning to choose or prefer. Essentially, the word is taken to mean the implication of intention or volition.

This is the first energy center presenting an ability to deal with and perceive life from an abstract perspective. This might be considered the "lower edges" of the higher mind. The word abstract comes from the 14th century Latin word *abstractus* "drawn away." It was also described as "withdrawn or separated from material objects or practical matters." Since the lower mind gains its strength and perspective from details, specifics and facts, we may assume that an abstract perspective is relective of the higher mind and might be more conceptual, interrelated, organizational and implied. It therefore participates in the world from a different perspective than the three "lower" center below the heart. Additionally, the action that takes place is much more internal. This is not to be confused with the idea of *locus of control*. It has less to do with motivation than it does with receiving information from sources other than the physical world. As the "lower" centers are much more *instinctive*, the "higher" centers are much more *intuitive*.

The words *instinct* and *intuition* have been used interchangeably by the majority of the world's population. The subtle difference in their meanings has escaped detection largely due to the fact that the commonly agreed upon validation of information we receive about our physical world must be based on physical clues, logic and rationalities, vis a' vis; *evidence* (from Latin *ex-* "out of, from" and *videre* "to see"). Validation based on "irrational" feeling is not acceptable *except* where there is a belief that there *is* a rational explanation but that we are just unable to "see" it at the moment. How far we will allow this point to be stretched, I believe, is just a matter of what personal reality is based on for each of us. If we belong to a scientific group, there is almost no "wiggle" room. If we belong to a religious group, anything connected to "faith" is acceptable. Essentially, it all boils down to our individual experience and the groups we choose to share our values with. However, this is not the difference I wish to clarify. The origins of the words give us the clues to their "true" meanings. Let's move on.

The word *instinct* comes from 15th century Latin *instinguere* meaning to "incite, impel." The word *incite* comes from 14th century Latin *incitare* "to put into rapid motion" and the word *impel* comes from 14th century Latin *impellere* "to push, drive forward or urge on." The quality of being an *innate tendency* originated in the 1560s as the Age of Reason began to attribute evidential causes for all physical phenomena while highlighting the senses (including the mind) and cementing all 16th century beliefs toward physical causes. All these factors have a component of urging one into physical action. This dimension of being physical is what connects *instinct* to the "lower" centers.

The word *intuition* comes from the 15th century Latin word *intueri* meaning "look at, consider" from *in-* "at, on" + *tueri* "to look at, watch over." The derivative 14th century Latin word *tutorem* adds the meaning of "guardian, watcher." Through these meanings we can see that the word *intuition* does not imply action, but merely observation and awareness. Action then becomes a matter of choice *not* reaction as would be that of instinct.

The next question that begs to be answered is look at and watch over who or what? The fact that the question is framed in "lower mind" vernacular (observer versus observed) gives us a hint as to how we must perceive the flashes of information from our *intuition* differently. I purposely used the word flashes to indicate how the information occurs. The term "watch over" carries with it the implication of a perspective superior to that of one where things are seen in terms of polarized parts. Our perception of the flash is composed of a fully integrated matrix of which we are a part. Differing from the temporal forces of the mind (past, present and future) the information or flash "arrives" fully integrated where, if we attempt to separate out the factors of its composition so the mind can reconstruct it into temporal language, we lose the continuity of the impression and the flash dissipates. We can compare this with attempting to describe a dream where we are confused by the time sequence of events within the dream. What came before? What came after? These questions force the experience into a format which lends itself to a linear continuity characteristic of mental functioning. The more we struggle to describe it by imposing the mind's temporal format, the more we dissipate the integrated timeless fabric and we lose the whole "thread" of the dream. It's much like attempting to describe a spider web to someone by only using on strand.

When we perceive something with the "lower mind," the dimension dominant in the lower centers, we perceive an experience *statically*; that is, in terms of parts, subject and object, before and after, with or without and in differing directions. When we perceive something through *intuition*, it's dynamic, moving and integrated. The "substance" of its existence is revealed through the style and flavor of its integration.

Essentially, when we have a flash of *intuition*, we perceive ourselves as part of the experience we are having through our perception and participation in it. If we choose to adjust our position within its matrix, we change the balance of components and reframe the experience by producing a different style of integration. We could compare this experience to playing an interactive computer game but where the programming for the integration would have to operate on a much more subtle and sophisticated level than any programmer could have ever dreamed. Simply put, when we adjustment ourselves, we change the balance of the game and reframe the experience for ourselves and anyone else involved. The key is that we are not changing something we "see" as from an observer's perspective but that in changing ourselves we change the overall experience. This is one of the dynamic principles of quantum physics; the observer influences and interacts with the observed.

Intuition operates on all three of the "upper" levels but grows perceptibly more subtle with each higher level. In comparison, think back to the analogy of the relationship between ice, water and vapor.

To understand the value of this type of perceiving we must first return to the mindset of the heart center individual. Since the heart center operates from the perspective of selflessness, we know that the possessive self absorption common to the solar plexus is absent and the individual is able to "listen" to what is outside of his own sphere of the self. His own interests no longer serve as a barrier to him being able to "hear" and "feel" the world. This will leave him perceiving the "flow" of the world but with no understanding of the bigger picture that he finds himself a part of. He still sees the "needs" of others as empty vessels needing to be filled. As the flashes of *intuition* from the throat center start to come into play, he is able to "feel" the larger picture and his opportunity to change it through his participation. This is the first place where the empathy of the heart has the opportunity to morph into active compassion. As he changes himself to fit the design of the *intuitive* impression the throat center has provided him with, he changes the immediate experience for himself and others through integrating the impression.

To see the difficulty of another human being, feel their pain but be able to let them struggle through it without interfering is an indication of throat center awareness provided that the withheld assistance does not emanate from fear, selfishness or indifference typical of the lesser qualities of the solar plexus or feeling responsible which is typical of the heart center. The throat center individual is aware of the necessity for the suffering person to experience the difficulty in order to come to a clearer realization of themselves. The throat center individual may appear to be devoid of any compassion to any observers which may serve to compound any sense of frustration they may feel in appearing cognitively dissonant as such to others. This awareness may be strictly *intuitive* or may have been understood but, in either case, the throat center individual has developed a trust in the *intangible* guidance of the upper centers. To see an example of this type of dynamic, the movie "The Razor's Edge" with Bill Murray illustrates a fine example of this learned "mindset" in relation to all the players.

The idea that direction comes from a place other than obvious physical factors is not a new idea. Spiritual disciplines and religions around the world have developed philosophies and path requirements in order to organize and explain this phenomenon. Ruumet (Ruumet, 2006) has called this "deflating needs for a purpose." This perspective asserts that each of us has an underlying "knowing" of the universe's web like matrix of "easily flowing" integration. That is, there is a "Tao" or natural way that energies move in order to produce and maintain the balance of natural forces. To stretch the point, we might even say that this indicates a tacit "destiny." Eastern philosophers also call this the "water course way." The premise is that, energy, as does water, follows the path of least resistance and that this path often runs contrary to any human desires based on evidential and mental validation. To take the position of this contrary direction is often called "pushing the river." The visual itself seems ludicrous but certainly conveys the futility of working against the natural order of things. When we encounter an individual who is "pushing the river" or as the Kabbalists put it, "following the path of severity," the individual vested in trusting their throat center orientation is able to "feel" where this person's action may lead them in the long run and encourages action that may appear to run contrary to what is desired but that will eventually cycle them through to a point of natural balance where a new awareness may be experienced. This bears a very close parallel to what has commonly been referred to as "tough love." This perspective allows the person who is being guided to choose action or inaction that will lead to undesirable personal stress producing consequences. It takes a great deal of trust and strength on the part of the throat center person to allow this person to "trip over their own feet" and possibly injure themselves while learning a life lesson where the heart center person would have simply "rescued" them or taken on the burden of the difficulties themselves to spare the inexperienced person the pain of their choices and the diminished quality of their interpersonal rapport. The short term "down side" for the throat center person may come from the advised person becoming initially angry at them for refraining from taking action on their behalf when they could have "helped." The long term "down side" for the heart center person is that the lesson needing to be learned will be delayed and the advised person will expect the heart center person to "rescue" them every time the circumstances reoccur. This effectively puts the heart center person into the position of being obligated to enable continued ignorance through interfering. We might also say that this might contribute toward enabling the advised person's *shadow*. However, though the circumstances may produce difficulty for the "helped" person in the long run, it still develops the spirit of giving, yielding and letting go in the heart center person. Each person learns their "lessons" through the actions or inactions of people operating on "higher" or "lower" levels.

To operate from the throat center yields a greater sense of "authenticity" than what occurs on the lower levels. Since the direction and impetus results from a place that is so obviously other than external in its influence, it gives us a sense of us "coming from" a totally and individually expressive perspective. This also resonates with Maslow's level of Actualization (Maslow, 1943) in that we are fulfilling a need to conform to a "wider order" of things or something that is much larger than us and more universal in its application. Although Maslow described it on a more individual scale, as for example, becoming a better parent, his focus can be expanded to a much wider view. This authenticity gives us the sense that we are contributing something to and resonating with the larger whole and thereby confirming our sense of self worth relative to the world in our own eyes. This is *not* to be confused with the pride which is so pervasive in the solar plexus individual equating to what we might call "spiritual bypass" which is a denser or grosser dynamic solidly grounded in seeking recognition through polarizing with the material world.

The issue of sex and the exchange of energy as perceived and generated through the throat center takes on a whole new dimension when we move from *instinct* to *intuition*. This difference in the quality of our perception readily lends itself to the practice of Tantric sex where the object of intercourse is not so much a question of sensuality (solar plexus) or a union through physical release (heart center) but one of building energy for endeavors much more inclusive than the simple release of physical tension or the expression of affection. The release simply results in neutralizing the differences in our personal energy potentials (For a better comprehension of this dynamic please refer back to the example of two containers in the In-tension section). An orgasm or climax acts as a "blitzkrieg" through bringing the energy differential to crescendo and releasing it as though it were a sudden lightning flash breaking down all barriers to the exchange. We feel "spent" after it occurs because it requires total focus to unify the energy in one direction. Once begun the energy becomes totally directed by our animal *instincts* and is almost irresistible. In Tantra, this release is withheld through discipline and great effort in overcoming our animal *instincts* and then sublimated toward spiritual pursuits that enable perception and power for dealing with the world through a broader awareness. Hence, the ultimate goal of its use is purported to be enlightenment.

So, as the heart center and throat center work together, the heart center contributes the "allowing" of compassion or *involuntary* empathy as described in the introduction and the throat center provides the direction needed through *intuition* and *volunteering* empathy, hence the will aspect, to resolve any imbalance in opposing polarities operating in the conflicting circumstances.

The fact that the throat center is representative of the "do" or will aspect of our inner nature asserts its contribution through providing the impetus to take the action we take when we trust on this level. However, the ability to "see" the matrix in its entirety comes from the center above; the third eye.

The Third Eye Center

The third eye center, or *Ajna* in Sanskrit, lies within the skull at the approximate location of the pituitary gland. To gauge where that is we can take an imaginary line from the place midway between the eyes and just above the brow (where the Indians indicate the spot with a red or black dot) to a point directly down from the top of the head. I hesitate to use the word crown as many people assume this is the spot on the upper back of the skull where the hair grows in a spiral. The *Ajna* center is the place where those participating in spiritual practice have focused their attention in order to develop a capacity for clairvoyance (clear seeing). Clairaudience (clear hearing) is a function of the throat center.

This is the second of the "upper centers." Where the throat center lends itself toward an *intuitive* understanding or "knowing" how all circumstances are integrated, the third eye allows a broader comprehension by allowing us to envision or *intuitively* "see" the complete matrix of energies involved. The perception of the third eye is intuitive but much more comprehensive than the throat center. A good analogy would be to compare a blind man with augmented tactile and auditory skills moving around a room with a sighted man who would have a clear "picture" of where everything was and know exactly where to focus energy and attention to move smoothly and easily within the furniture patterns of the room. The blind man's movements would be more approximate than the sighted man and he would have probably learned to "tap into" the energy flow or "feng shui" of the room. Overall the sighted man would have a much fuller comprehension of the energies involved in the room through his ability to actually "see."

Where the heart center is indicative of letting go and the throat center "obliquely" suggests that we follow the path of least resistance relative to the natural order of things, the third eye center encourages us to acknowledge the fact that we have no control over anything (Ruumet, 2006) save ourselves and even in that our free will is limited depending on what we have done to our physical bodies over our lifetime. In health, there is a point where we are no longer willing or able to reverse the damage we might have done through poor choices. In the interest of conserving energy or being able to continue our lessons under renewed circumstance it is sometimes wiser to regroup by discorporating and starting again. This mortality factor is enmeshed with third eye energy in that the ability to envision the entire matrix of life encourages much more trust and comfort in the individual concerning his future passing and the fact that he will still have other opportunities to gain awareness as he follows the path of least resistance in allowing himself to flow *with* the natural death and rebirth cycle rather than resist it which is usually the case with lower centers. The idea of reincarnation may be objectionable to some, but please remember, we are examining the perspectives gained through the spiritual beliefs over the centuries by a multitude of cultures that have developed disciplines for ascending through the chakras. This understanding and belief often "comes with the territory." Whatever beliefs you may hold about where you go when you pass, all scriptures talk about a resurrection in one form or another. It doesn't necessarily have to include a prophet or a deity even though most do.

The third eye is generally the pathway in which visions and intuitive flashes come to those who put themselves into a meditative state or those who have enough self discipline to simply clear their mind and contemplate. They come when the mind is free of clutter and the day to day issues that arouse the lower mind are not demanding attention. This state of "calm water" is encouraged by disciplines similar to Zen and Buddhism in order to reach a state of "enlightenment" which, simply put, is coming to a place of acceptance and understanding of how "things are," letting material day to day concerns freely "flow by" and comprehending our place in the world.

The third eye also reflects a quality of "undoing" (Ruumet, 2006). On first perusal we could assume that this might be an individual's ability to do harm to himself. But on closer examination we may come to see that having a panoramic view of our perceived reality gives us an unprecedented ability to "see" the consequences of our actions before they occur. This is not to say that we have the ability for precognition as much as a type of awareness enabling us to comprehend the outcome of actions as a function of our ability to understand and envision the natural flow of energies in the dynamic interplay of life circumstances. In perceiving this way we are able to recognize what appear to be the beginnings *and* endings of chosen actions with equal alacrity as a complete and balanced matrix, free of the time constraints that normally bind individuals operating on the lower levels. We, essentially, see events as having no beginning and no end but simply an inter-relative balance of forces all occurring *at the same time*. Seeing events in this way is in keeping with perceiving *intuitively* rather than logically or *instinctually*. Perhaps *this* is the basis for what is defined as precognition. "Seeing" the future is just "seeing" another part of the matrix.

Those who are still operating within the perceptual limits of the lower centers are generally not able to conceive of, let alone utilize, operating from an *intuitive* perspective rather than mental or *instinctual* unless they have regressed from a higher level due to ego issues that have yet to be worked through totally. The person who has *not* yet arrived at the upper operative levels only sees reality through a reflection of their desires with no allowance for the unexpected outcomes or natural flows of energy inherent in their learning process. The person who *has arrived* but regressed will have a vague perception that something might be different with what they have perceived but be unable to "put their finger on it."

Polarized or acquisitive motives create such a gross and obtrusive effect that the gentler aspects of *intuition* are unable to penetrate the borders of the tangible mind until the mind has either lost its command of our perceived reality through trauma or has been subdued by an activity such as meditation or a peak experience.

There is one more point to ponder. The heart is the balance point between the upper centers and the lower centers. It is the point where we "cross over" from being directed by the tangible world to being directed by the inner or intangible world. Essentially, we can sat that this is the point where our awareness crosses over from an external *locus of control* to an internal *locus of control;* from rational to irrational; from material to energetic. This is not to say that the lower centers are voided as the upper centers "take over." It just indicates that the overall directivity has shifted its point of reference for what we accept as our reality. When the bible says we can either worship god or mammon, it is essentially asking if we are motivated by the material world or the energetic world. Both the upper centers and the lower centers participate equally but one or the other must "direct."

The Crown Center

The crown center, or *Sahasrara* in Sanskrit, lies approximately two inches above the skull in a direct line above the pineal gland. Note that it is *outside* the body. This emphasizes the fact that this center is essentially beyond the scope of human understanding. If we look at the pictures of ancient wisdom figures such as Jesus, Buddha, Krishna, Mohammad, we will see what has commonly been called a halo. The implication is that these individuals operated on a level much more subtle than any of the other centers and that their physical existence was of no import except as a vehicle for the expression of *their perception* of universal energy. As individuals, we may, at short intervals, "glimpse" the consciousness and awareness existing at this level but I believe that no on in the world, save for a few enlightened souls, operates from this perspective. Yet, I will say that this is a primary entry and exit point for energy as is the perineum relative to the root center. These two points can be loosely compared to the extremes of yin and yang where the type of manifestation is almost purely material or energy. The yin and yang interplay with its infinitely possible combinations of energy acts through *all* the centers of the body in varying degrees and combinations. Hence, the variety and the diversity of life expression.

It would be pointless to attempt to describe types of perception or uses of energy in that the crown center includes them all in an unfathomable fashion except through the awareness of a few enlightened souls. And, even then, who would they be able to explain it to that would have any comprehension or comparable experience to relate with?

BIG EGO AND LITTLE EGO

In this day and age the word *ego* has taken on a meaning very different from what was originally intended by the growing psychological movement of the beginning of the twentieth century. To express a sense of *ego* in our contemporary vernacular is to assume that one is speaking of pride or conceit. The word *ego* originates from the Latin word *ego* simply meaning "I or self." It also dates back to Old English in 1714 as a metaphysical term meaning "transcending the physical" or, in this case, more than the self. The word began its association with psychology in 1894. It gained the most power in being viewed as pride or conceit in 1969 when the phrase "ego trip" became popular.

In terms of psychology, the meaning takes on a flavor that is a bit more complicated, yet, still deals with a more or less "factual" basis. The Penguin Dictionary of Psychology states, "In classical theory the ego represents a cluster of cognitive and perceptual processes including memory, problem-solving, reality-testing, inference-making and self-regulated striving, that are conscious and in touch with reality, as well as specific defence mechanisms that serve to mediate between the primitive instinctual demands of the id, the internalized social, parental inhibitions and prohibitions of the superego, and the knowledge of reality" (Reber, Allen and Reber, 1985). With more brevity we could say that from a psychological perspective the *ego* acts as a director integrating our perception of ourselves through our thoughts, feelings and worldly experiences. By virtue of the fact that the field of psychology is still pressing to define itself in terms of facts relative to the physical world we can say that it will primarily operate within the boundaries of the three lower centers. However, there are those of us that are attempting to retain the boundaries of its expanded definition by including perspectives common to humanistic and transpersonal views and, therefore, moving toward intangible viewpoints common to the three upper centers. We must also remember, however, that the heart center is still the mediator between the upper and lower three centers and operates "straddling" both.

Having suggested these parameters, I will use little *"ego"* when I refer to a perspective held by the lower mind and its "factual" requirements and motivations and a capitalized ego or *"Ego"* when I refer to perspectives that allow for direction motivated by more intangible or intuitive sources indicative of activities directed by the upper centers.

When we speak of *ego*, we refer to an investment into preference and performance as a reflection of our striving for recognition and validity in the eyes of others. The need for recognition and validity often emanates from the absence of encouragement or validation of personal value that comes as a result of not being accepted as we are by the caretakers that raised us. When this acceptance is not given us as a child, we often spend the rest of our lives, either consciously or unconsciously, compensating for what we feel we have been deprived of...acceptance as a unique person. This solidly inserts the *ego* as our prime motivator beneath every action we take or refrain from taking in our daily living. By believing this perception of ourselves, we assert to ourselves that we are neither valid nor acceptable as we are. This makes us almost totally susceptible to the flexible tides and opinions of the external world.

When dealing with the world from the perspective of *ego,* our impression of ourselves can change in an instant depending on who we are talking to and who they may remind us of from our past. This lack of acceptance is the most potent root of our *toxic shame*. By accepting this "deficient" perspective of ourselves we are at the mercy of the opinions of the external world leaving us subservient to an external *locus of control*. When we focus on what we believe we lack, we only serve to intensify the feeling. The Chinese say, "To focus on your enemy gives them power."

It is said that we are all reflections of each other; that we see ourselves in the responses of others. So, what if we start this process by beginning "at a perceived deficit" through compensating for what we *feel* we lack? What does the response that we receive mean to us? It only serves to generate a response that *confirms* the held belief of being "invalid, unworthy and deficient." The bible says, "As a man thinketh, so is he." If this truly is the case, why not think a different thought? Why not fake it til we make it? Why? Because in our hearts we know the statement is a lie. Yet, the belief of "inferiority" that generated it is also a lie. So, how do we approach "repairing" our self concept to a condition of "I'm okay as I am" if we can't directly address it without reconfirming its effects?

This approach has created a dilemma that the therapeutic world has been dealing with since its beginnings. It is based on and supports the human instinct to fight or resist what is undesirable. In adding energy to any difficult situation, especially to resistance, it only serves to exacerbate the conflict. One of Newton's laws governing physics says that every action taken produces and equal and opposite reaction. So, if we add energy, or in this case attention, to either side of a polarity, the law of physics responds by creating an equal and opposite energy to rebalance the polarity. An analogy might be a physical tug of war between people. After adding more people to one side, to equalize the energy, we must add more people to the opposing side. Hence, more people produce a larger conflict.

We've seen the same type of action occurring in any war. One side attempts to overpower the other and the other, naturally, responds instinctively with a larger force to repel the invader. This strategy increases the intensity of the conflict by involving more people on both sides and escalating the conflict through a "see-saw" effect. This is also excruciatingly evident in the Middle East.

So, through this analogy to our psychological battle of using compensation we can see that it will only serve to intensify the original assumption; the belief of having a deficient self through attracting equal and opposite opinions and responses that confirm that belief.

The *ego's* need to control is evident through all these interactions. The competition for dominance in nature is evident everywhere we look. The *ego* is the mind's contender for answering this struggle. The senses, including the mind, are the representatives and vehicles for perceiving with our animal nature. However, our contemporary view of ourselves posits the mind as being "above" this nature. Perhaps this is another compensation for the belief that this part of our nature is unacceptable or deficient in light of our utopian objectives. Yet, the animal part of our nature supplies the momentum toward every action we take as a response to the information generated by those six senses (the mind included). However, is this all there is to us? Are we only animals acting out a perpetual struggle? Many of us in our modern day approach to and understanding of life certainly think so. If polarity is truly in play, is there another part of our nature that struggles *against* this influence?

Much like our *instinctive* and animal natures that operate by constantly adjusting and rebalancing the competition between differing physical, emotional and mental polarities, the *intuitive* side of our nature also maintains a balance between itself and that *instinctive* nature. Both are needed to maintain the flow of life through adding insight by virtue of experiencing the field of change between them. Our *ego* may be compared to our *instinctive* nature and or *Ego* may be compared to our *intuitive* nature.

In our current day attitudes and beliefs there is a bias in navigating the "space" between these two capacities created by our insecurities (*ego*). The New Age movement AND our religious tenets have suggested that in order to be "spiritual" we must deny the animal side of our nature in favor of living wholly according to prescribed non-tangible concepts. Perhaps this is an attitude suggestive of *Thanatos* or our attempt to escape the suffering that is an inherent component of the physical world. The Easterners call this "place" we desire to escape to *Nirvana* and the Westerners call it *Heaven*. For many of us struggling with difficult times, this type of oblivion definitely has its attractions even though our scriptures "dress up" these existences with components of angelic eternity and eternal peace to give us a conceptual frame that we can comprehend and yearn toward. Our cultures, most assuredly including our religions, profess the path to it as leading a blameless life thereby becoming our "ticket" to entering. However, the persisting bottom line of pursuing this track is that we, essentially, have *created* the belief that it is necessary for us to deny our physical or animal nature in order find peace. Yet, the universe goes on whether we choose to be aware of its patterns of polarity or not. Neither the hedonistic (*ego*) nor the "spiritual" (*Ego*) sides of attitude are any better or any worse than each other. *Both* are needed to exist in balance. We need to accept both of these natures within us in order that we may "feel whole." If we deny either perspective, we relegate it to becoming an unconscious *shadow* and then find ourselves feeling that something is missing.

So, with understanding the effect of our human bias, we can see from a universal perspective that these two directions of energy are a natural interplay in a larger field of polarities. To deny one or the other is to obscure the awareness we need that gives us a sense of "wholeness." This field can be compared to the ocean that the fish exists in. For the fish to deny the existence of water, or land, would be ludicrous and most certainly limit its options in living a "full" fishy life. But, isn't that just what we're doing when we deny the physical or we deny the intangible? By recent examples, India has historically lived a life geared toward the spiritual and has endured abject poverty. The west has live almost exclusively through the material and feels unsatiated and "hungry." (Perhaps for the west this may be a prime mover for "emotional eating?") Both cultures have recently moved toward incorporating a bit of each other. As a result, the abject poverty of India seems to be abating and the existential loneliness of the west is beginning to make us feel more "included" in the universe.

For us, which we are motivated by, *ego* or *Ego*, is not important. What *is* important is that we are *aware* of which we are motivated by and having an awareness of the lessons that each presents us. The most important aspect of awareness is allowing ourselves to accept and experience what comes to us without attempting to alter it to our preference. This runs completely contrary to our historically western way of doing things. However, the last half of the twentieth century has found us welcoming eastern disciplines, such as Zen, promoting the concept of emptying the mind, thereby reducing our instinctual tendency toward resistance and diffusing our need for control. Yet, importing these disciplines still brings with them seemingly resistance oriented practices such as Kung Fu, Karate and other martial arts that emphasize dominance while only paying lip service to the more peaceful Zen like philosophies that may reside behind them.

The qualities of competition and urge toward dominance are most certainly powerful factors directing our animal nature. I am not suggesting that we eliminate these urges as this would only feed into the tendency to bury part of our consciousness. What I *am* suggesting, however, is to move toward placing more emphasis on the *Ego* or *intuitive* side of our nature in an effort to establish more of a balance between these two opposing urges. When the water is free of waves and ripples, we can"see" much more clearly what motivations reside beneath our actions.

Putting more emphasis on the *Ego* side of our nature is not necessarily always the best perspective in light of the fact that it has its own pitfalls relative to maintaining a balance. In some cases it may appear that *intuition* is the dominating motivation, yet, other motivations may be in play. Let's follow some history and then an example.

The sensuality movement of the sixties contained an emphasis on a "live and let live" philosophy accompanied by a disdain of the predominating conventional "American Dream" philosophy encouraging our *egotistic* or *instinctually* competitive nature of "getting ahead" or coming out "on top." This portion of the population, then called the "establishment," was indicative of the struggle for dominance so common to our repressed animal nature. Yet, the aspect of sensuality that was so typical of the "Hippie" movement was also indicative of that same animal nature but a part that had become considered taboo to admit a yearning for by the existing culture. This and the LSD craze spearheaded by Timothy Leary only served to give form to our unconscious desire to be free of our socialized *egotistic* or *instinctual* urges and become more attentive to things much less tangible. An aspect of "letting go" was inherent in the budding drug culture. This most certainly drew sharp criticism from the existing culture as embodying laziness and withdrawal from socially sanctioned attitudes even in the face of repressed desires wishing to be able to do the same. However, in spite of the fact that the attitude was drug oriented and anti-establishment, it *did* allow a break from the typical materialistic western focus and allowed movement toward creating a space for the *intuitive* side of our nature to have breathing room and to begin to provide an opportunity for the relationship between *instinctual* and *intuitive* to be brought back into balance.

As the "Hippie" movement began to dwindle, a new movement began to fill the increasing gap. This was the New Age movement. It entered the scene with principles that carried on the diminishing of our ingrained addiction to a materialistic attitude toward life, science being its dominant champion, toward a more intangible focus but with less of the rebellious attitude so prevalent in the demeanor of the sixties movement participants. I hesitate to use the word *spiritual* as the descriptor as the word has become so distorted by contemporary misunderstanding that it allows assumptions that pigeon hole its meaning, especially, by those who might harbor religious leanings. Yet, today contemporary religion has claimed some of the older supporters of the movement. Some may say that the New Age began in the sixties but I feel that what it has morphed into promotes a more gentle approach, prevalent in the movement today, through slowly growing free of the animosity of the times. In its current manifestation we can more clearly see the differing motivations inherent in being part of the movement.

In any movement there are always rules; spoken and unspoken. Each person will incorporate these rules in their lifestyle, consciously or unconsciously, through adjusting them to fit what they either believe or desire their lifestyle to be. So, regardless as to whether the rules are specific or general, the bottom line for their incorporation into our lives rests with us. Hence, comparable to religious organizations, we may have factions that are "orthodox" and others that are "relaxed" in their application of the rules. Even though the New Age movement has no central "head" or director as does conventional religion, the rules and codes of behavior are still understood or misunderstood depending on the person's level of emotional maturity and incorporation of the principles. Let's follow an example.

Compassion is a concept and principle supported by both religion and the New Age movement. To have feelings for and a willingness to assist others in life's difficulties is an expected behavior for one who adheres to the advertised principles of both. This type of behavior is mostly a product of our *intuitive* and humanitarian natures. Additionally, if our needs for survival have been met, especially from the perspective of Maslow's Hierarchy of Needs, we will be more likely to follow it. Yet, our natural animal *instincts* will still lead us to first consider how beneficial compassion will be to our current status of survival in the world we participate in. If our *instincts* are stronger than our *intuitive* nature, our choice of behavior will be more geared toward our survival. If our *intuitive* nature is stronger than our *instinctual* nature, and this will be more likely if Maslow's needs have been met, our choice of behavior will be more geared toward compassion.

So, our first factor dealing with our motivation is dependent on whether our survival needs have been met. This diminishes the intensity of our *instinctual* nature and allows more of our *intuitive* nature to be felt and expressed. But we must remember that Maslow's Hierarchy of Needs not only applies to physical survival but emotional survival as well. In some cases our physical needs may be met but our emotional or belonging needs may not. In these cases it is very likely that the need to belong or *to be seen* as belonging will lead one to proffer lip service toward compassionate or intuitive feelings yet perform actions that may reflect a continued attitude toward supporting a personally oriented survival demeanor. In a more blunt fashion we may say that this represents the Sunday Christian who, after mass, rejoins the community and slanders or steals from another church member or the New Age advocate professing peace, love and unity that also slanders their neighbor's dedication and steals from them in an effort to compensate for feelings of shame, unworthiness or inferiority. Unfortunately, to show support for a group with the goal of being accepted by them through demeaning participants who don't appear to live by *our* interpretation of group rules is one of the most unhealthy foundations in which to grow esteem within a group. Almost always, the need to protect the lie becomes more important than improving the quality of the group leading them to fall subject to what they have accused others of. This was most evident in medieval history during the times of the inquisition where taking sides for personal gain often backfired with the accuser "getting eaten" by bigger fish.

As long as we are incarnate or living in these physical bodies our existence and awareness resides in a field composed of the balance between our survival and *instinctual* nature, or *ego*, and our humanitarian and *intuitive* nature or *Ego*. To say that any one polarity should have a substantial dominance over the other is inviting conflict and difficulty, especially, since the tendency of the universe seems to move toward balancing polarities. However, with the current emphasis on survival being the dominant force in the world, it is necessary to temporarily weight our *intuitive* side more heavily in order to bring a more balanced world perspective. Once the polarities come near to being balanced, it is my feeling that a slight edge leaning toward *Ego* or the *intuitive* would be beneficial by keeping us aware of what might be needed to assist the world toward moving into a more compassionate and cooperative attitude. In New Age perspectives, it is believed by its scholars that the world has spent enough time in the *instinctual* or material side to complete what is necessary for our human evolution and that to develop our *intuitive*, intangible and spiritual side is what is necessary to complete a much larger evolutionary cycle toward universal "wholeness." It is my belief that religions have long ago lost the understanding of the larger scale of things in favor of a literal acceptance of current scriptures. In much simpler terms, at this point in our evolutionary growth, it would be best if the mind's practicalities became subservient to the heart's direction. Absorption and preoccupation with details only serves to cater to our *instinctual* need for control and distracts us from the promptings of our heart. The old saying that proffers this is, "The longest journey is from the head to the heart."

THE ROAD TO REBALANCE

BALANCE is DIFFERENT for EVERYONE

To assume that the balance point for health is the same for everyone is not only foolish but presumptuous. Do our genes produce the same characteristics in everyone? Of course not. Is our mood and energy level always the same? No again. Just as the earth goes through day and night and the tides ebb and flow, so do we. So how, then, do we determine what being healthy really is? We must look at something which is immeasurable, indefinable and has no scientific standard for comparison. This question follows our most changeable quality. How do we feel?

So, right now you're thinking, "How I feel is no gauge as to whether I'm healthy or not. That's just my mood." On the surface this seems quite logical and shows common sense. But your statement only shows how much we have entrusted our well being to people who we believe know better what is in our best interest than we do. Concerning some aspects of the workings of our body, this may be true. But as a general rule, the best person to know what's happening in our body is us. Why do we not acknowledge that this is a function of our exaggerated focus on what is outside of us? Because we have been trained that what is important for our survival comes from others; that our *intuition* about people and situations is not to be trusted. Right now you're saying, "But what about our animal instincts?" And you'd be right. But what we have defined as our animal *instincts* are actually the workings of our mind. Our true animal *instincts* we have repressed and distanced ourselves from. We have misinterpreted and accepted the *instinctual* workings of our mind as *being* our animal *instinct*. If you don't believe this, ask yourself what happens when your dog or cat becomes ill? What do they do? They go off by themselves, crawl up in a ball and go to sleep. The only thing they eat or drink is water. *Instinctively* (and this is certainly *animal instinct*) they know that withdrawing and allow the body to fix itself is what is necessary for them to *feel* better. What do humans do? We first get angry at ourselves believing that we have been exposed to some outside germ or bacteria that has attacked us, believing that it is *they* who have made us sick and then run to another person (most likely a doctor) to fix what *we* have done to ourselves. Don't get me wrong. There are some times where illness and injury are so severe that we *do* need an outside source to assist us because we have damaged ourselves past our ability to fix it by ourselves. Yet, even the circumstances that we have created in those issues are based on some judgment we made about either actions we did or didn't take leading to that injury or dietary, sleep or exercise needs that we ignored when our body was screaming to us about what it required. Did we listen? No. We did what our *mind* told us to do rather than what our *feelings* told us. Our emotions follow the same progression of events. We feel bad. We *think* about why we feel bad. We use those thoughts to qualify our feelings and then create emotions. Then, every time our emotions are triggered we blame outside sources for the way we feel. Are you starting to see a pattern? Where is our accountability for what we feel? For most of us, it rests outside ourselves. So what is it that we call it when we allow the surrounding circumstances to dictate how we run our lives? It is considered an external *locus of control*. How did we come to trust in it? By being taught that what we feel is not valid. Our feelings and *intuition* have become buried in the facts, figures and justifications for what we do. We have become disconnected from the most important indicator of our well being; how we feel.

Even though not acknowledging our feelings and *intuition* is a common thread within the average western population, we must remember that everyone will be different in how we submerge our sensitivities and to what degree. A person who is more aware (not mature) in their development will obviously deal with these sensitivities in a more conscious, in the moment and "above board" fashion. Those who are more fearful and less acquainted with their *shadow* will be more oblivious to their *intuitive* sensitivities resulting in more defensive posturing, often, to the point of denial. I hesitate to use the word *mature* as it has taken on more than a double meaning in our culture. For those who are *instinctual* and "evidence based" and firmly rooted in the field of polarities in their perception of "reality," the word has a social meaning that relates to dealing with tasks in an accountable manner or in a socially prescribed fashion that produces a polarized consistency in daily circumstances. This insures a sense of security throughout our lifestyle. Growing, evolving and becoming more *intuitive* is seen as behaving irrationally and "upsetting the applecart." Requiring people to actually take each situation in their daily lives as a new experience runs contrary to the contemporary belief that the consistency in our conception of security is what produces happiness and safety. For those of us who are more embracing of our *intuitive* and feeling natures (not emotional) and reside more in the chakras from the heart center and above, we will see maturity as "in the moment" awareness that allows more of the world to penetrate our lives as it is, rather than what we might think that it "should" be. Please remember that feelings occur in the moment and emotion is the result of how we frame those feelings with the mind in order to program our future behavior to either embrace or avoid a repeated experience. This programming tendency is a function of the solar plexus and below and how we have categorized the feelings we've felt in the past.

The major reason why so many of us are so petrified of our feelings is that they arise within us of, what seems to be, their own volition. To us, we assume that they are uncontrollable. They just occur. Feelings of joy, contentment, excitation and other preferable feelings are openly accepted by most people unless there is an overpowering sense of guilt connected to having them. In that case they are treated in the same way that undesirable feelings are handled. In this, it is my feeling that our *shadow* is the most important contributing force to their eruptions and the ultimate destination for them after they are handled by the *ego*. The more *shadow* we harbor, the more intensely we feel and fear it. *Shadow* is a result of our polarizing on the solar plexus level according to our preferences; conscious or unconscious. The *shadow's* champions are resistance, rationalization, projection, reaction formation, displacement, dissociation, denial and other defense mechanisms; some pathological, some immature and some neurotic. As we move to reside in the higher centers, much of our *shadow* has been or is in process of being surfaced and reintegrated with our *Ego*. The key to how it is handled rests with whether we are directed by the *Ego* or the *ego*. The *Ego* directs us to accept experience as it is, allowing it to remain in consciousness and is integrated. The *ego* uses defense mechanisms to submerge the unpleasant experience from the conscious mind, relegating it to *shadow*, thereby, intensifying its overall effect.

The act of *accepting* an experience and its attending feeling as it is, preferable or not, is staggering in the simplicity of its potential effect. The moment that *toxic shame* begins to have a foot hold, a *shadow* is created as the receptacle for all the unwanted feelings and experiences contributing to the chosen belief of one having an unacceptable self image. We can then say that the process of rebalancing consists of reintegrating what we have relegated to *shadow* with our openness and awareness. To have the awareness that this produces makes our ability to *accept* all parts of life "as it comes" paramount to maintaining health. In other words, the first step toward learning compassion must be the total acceptance of what we become aware of.

When we submit to the belief of our being unacceptable as we are, we lose the ability to have compassion. The feeling of unacceptability leads us to becoming defensive and preoccupied with our self image, thereby, making us unwilling and, perhaps, unable to focus on the needs and feelings of others. In becoming absorbed by what we *believe* other people think about us, we are no longer listening and accepting the world as it is.

Compassion is blocked. The heart center "shuts down" and we relegate ourselves to residing in the lower centers in the domain of the *ego*. When we allow life to come at us as it is and accept it as it is, we open the heart center, enable our ability to feel compassion and choose to reside in the domain of the *Ego*.

THE FIRST STEP: ACCEPTANCE

So, the first step in rebalancing ourselves is *acceptance*; to *accept* life as it is; not what it used to be (past), should be or could be (future), but *as it is*. In this, we have done the unthinkable. We have taken control away from the mind by removing its ability to use the time line as its foundation; the dimension necessary for the mind to operate. It's important to note here that the *shadow* is produced within the timeline by the *ego* as a precautionary measure meant to regulate future circumstances in order to prevent the exposure of our *toxic shame* and all the limitations it brings with it. If we are in the moment, there is no way to compare so shame has no footing.

The second step is the most crucial whether we are working on the *shadow* or not. It will change every other aspect of how we approach life. That is one of accountability.

THE SECOND STEP: ACCOUNTABILITY

When we hear the word *accountable* we, almost by mental *instinct*, substitute the word blame. In comparing against the old saying "fix the problem, not the blame" we have an important insight into our western mind. Since we are so scientific and oriented toward attributing cause and effect, we naturally ascribe blame as we would, just as easily, ascribe cause to an observed event. However, there is a distinction between cause and blame that is mostly unspoken and often unrealized. Cause is more often attributed to what *began* an occurrence and blame is attributed to who and what must be dealt with *after* an event has occurred. There is another lesser realized distinction. And that is that cause is mostly ascribed to inanimate events and blame is ascribed to human and animal events (those who have no reverence for animal life will also consider it causal). Do we really perceive that much of a difference? We may ascribe blame or cause to any events we wish but the plain truth is it is still perceived in a way that offers nothing toward changing the events it has propagated; just a need for someone to do the "cleanup." But even here we slide back into the timeframe domain of the mind. Blame and cause are still part of looking at life in a timeline; what occurred *before* and what occurred *after* present perceptions. If we accept life "as it comes" we cannot ascribe linear time qualities to being in the moment.

On first glance you would be saying, "But not to look at the past and the future is irresponsible." In our current culture this makes perfect sense. But what would you actually be saying in relation to contemporary thinking? In this framework, being responsible is accepting the potential for blame if the circumstance turns out badly for the people you are being responsible to. Let's first look at the meaning for *accountable*, then *blame* and then *cause* to gain a deeper understanding of the perceptions that they bring.

The earliest record of the word *accountability* comes from the 1300s Old French word *acont* meaning "reckoning of money received and paid." Obviously, with the suffix *–ability* we're referring to someone's potential to respond with a payment. So, the inference here is that if we hold someone *accountable* we feel that we are owed something and we expect to receive some form of payment from them.

The words *blame* and *blasphemy* seem to have both come into use in the 12th century from the Latin *blastemare* and *blasphemare* and modern French *blamer* relating to "revile, reproach, rebuke, reprimand, condemn and criticize." There seemed to develop some discrepancy as to their use and specific meaning through becoming interchangeable in their applications. In the way that contemporary culture adopts and morphs words to reflect differing intentions, perceptions and fads, even today, the evasiveness of their meanings will come as no surprise to us.

The word *cause* etymologically relates to legal implications suggesting idealistic reasons for taking actions. Hence, it can be connected to *before* and event has occurred. Unfortunately, its origins are unknown. In our current vernacular, it relates to urges toward initiating action directed by motivations, purposes and intended "end" results. Only in this light can it be interpreted as bringing about actions or circumstances as dictionary definitions seem to indicate. But still, it is time constricted in its meaning and, hence, only meaningful relative to the mind.

So to clarify, to be *accountable* is to be liable for starting and/or finishing an event. So now we face another dilemma. It's one thing not to feel responsible for an event and another to feel it and deny it. This conundrum is best exemplified in the Samurai culture. The word *giri* (pronounced gidee) is roughly defined as an obligation. One of the best expansions of perceiving the concept can be seen in the movie "Yakuza" (1975) where the character Tanaka Ken (a modern day samurai) *owes*

Harry Kilmer (American soldier) a "debt which he can never repay" for saving his wife and daughter during the post-war occupation in Japan. Their discussions revolve around the intensity with which the Japanese culture (specifically the samurai) feels the weight of a debt or accountability and the lack of the feeling and intensity that westerners acquiesce to. The most striking point brought up by Tanaka Ken was that if you feel the obligation, then you have it. If you don't feel the obligation, you do not. At this point we should also acknowledge that, like compassion, obligation or accountability are learned responses. If we haven't learned it, what recourse does the person who feels we are indebted to have? Our prison system and the character traits of its inmates (or lack of) is testimony to this dilemma. Do we train people to feel remorse after the fact? Will they learn? Is it up to us to teach them? Is it moral to force them to feel responsible for their actions? These questions are still being debated by people of differing chosen beliefs.

So, at this point you're probably asking, "Where are you going with this?" The point I would like to emphasize is that we must be *accountable* to ourselves first before we consider the "moral" expectations of others. However, in our culture a religious double standard comes into play. Contemporary interpretations of religious tradition would have that we must first be accountable to others before we "indulge ourselves." Yet, the bible and other scriptures encourage us "to thine own self be true." But what part of "thine own self" are we being true to? Is it our polarized physical existence which operates in the timeline dimensions of the mind and our lower centers or the timeless dimension of our *intuition* and the voice that emanates from our higher centers? Our "answer" resides in our ability to balance the two and live within the appearance of inequities and paradoxes as perceived by others.

Relative to accountability, we have gone all over the map. With so many perspectives on how to relate to it, is it any wonder how much confusion can result if even only between two people? It almost seems as if all of us might have a "claim" on everyone else's actions. And, in a way, this is true in that every action that is taken by an individual has an effect on everyone else even if only in a miniscule way. We must remember that in quantum physics any action that a participant takes in a field of experience, let alone an observer, changes the overall experience for everyone connected. An interesting movie that elaborates this perspective is "The Sound of Thunder" (2004) where the course of evolution takes a dramatic turn as the result of the death of one butterfly echoes the story about the butterfly flapping his wings and being felt on the other side of the globe.

So after all this we *still* need a working definition of what *accountability* will mean to us for the foundational and essential work we must do on ourselves in order to become balanced in our approach to our world. *Accountability* is our acceptance of life as it is without focus as to where the circumstances came from or who is to blame and without focus on what it should or could be given alternate circumstances. Additionally, any situation we may find ourselves in, desirable or not, is the result of some choice(s) *we* have made along the way. In this way we must apply ourselves toward being as aware as we are able. In this definition there is no "payment" implied as this is simply a full and open acknowledgement of our present situation and the extent of our involvement in it. The important component of this for us to understand is that this *accountability* and acknowledgement *is for us* not for the placation of the emotional security and perceived indebtedness that others might be comforted by. This may be a strange concept to wrap our head around but for many people a sense of worth and superiority comes from others being indebted to them; as subconscious and unacknowledged as that feeling might be that we may have buried it to. Extorting a feeling of personal worth through the forced manipulation of others serves as an unconscious confirmation of our feeling of worthlessness. Some of us are so fully absorbed with extorting respect, acknowledgement and obligation from others that we never realize that it might be being freely given had we allowed the situation to run its course without our coercion. In the long run, and again, the need for this type of manipulation only serves to confirm our feeling of unworthiness.

So now we have *acceptance* and *accountability* as being the first building blocks toward a healthy self concept.

THE THIRD STEP: AWARENESS

This next step requires us to look at and discriminate what choices have led us to arrive at our current situation(s). It also requires us to examine our preferences and understand what the motivations for them are. This is more easily said than done in that it is extremely easy to rationalize or justify our need to continue in the perception and the direction that has led to them. The mind has the ability, and very often uses it, to make the line very thin between what we have anticipated gaining from the situation and what is actually necessary to be in line with the natural forces. The key is that the natural forces are not personal; that is, there is no *ego* involved. Our focus must be applied to what is *necessary*, not preferred, to be in alignment with our *intuition* as opposed to maintaining a sense of control. Whatever age we are, the *ego* has had as many years to learn the buttons and switches, internal and external, which will encourage us to lean more toward a survival oriented approach; survival being the operative word and approach being the *ego's* defensive method. The stronger and more deeply entrenched our *shadows* are, the more difficult this will be. It is so very important that we are aware of our *shadow* and the defense mechanisms that protect them.

The objective of the manner of awareness that I am proposing is three fold. First, that we continually put the effort into "routing out" or bringing to light and reintegrating the *shadows* that we have already in place, second, that we are aware of our defense mechanisms as they present themselves toward defending those *shadows* and third, that we pick an endeavor in which to apply our energy that has *not been involved* in the production of *toxic shame*.

The act of being alert and aware at all times, by itself, is a challenging experience in that our natural human tendency is to put behaviors in place that will "handle life automatically" or without us paying attention and investing energy that we may want to apply to more pleasurable activities. This results in our consciousness remaining "asleep" as we move through life reacting to patterns that we have put into place that, over time, may have outlived their usefulness, yet, where we are still "programmed" to perform and react to them. It is also fertile ground for the defense mechanisms defending our *shadow* to easily slip into place while we let the acknowledgement of our awareness of them "slip by." We can view this as our tendency to "play dumb" when there's something we might not want to deal with due to the time and effort required while committing to future changes that might have to be maintained. Case in point; if we have not changed the way we react as a child to our fathers as we grow older, that is as an authority figure, we will find ourselves looking at every male who enters our life has having "dominion" over who we are and what we do. This is a great way of absolving ourselves of being *accountable* for our choices through letting someone else make them for us. More commonly, when men look at women as "mommy" and women look at men as "daddy", the emotional problems and complications resulting in ensuing male / female relationships are often catastrophic. Reassessing ourselves and changing our rapport with our opposite sex parent is necessary and a natural part of growing up. This type of "cross" relationship rapport is typical of what is dealt with in Transactional Analysis. It is, also, one of the major concepts underlying our culture's modern movement toward becoming personally responsible and *accountable*. The exploration of variations of this type of rapport and its implications can be best found in the books "Games People Play" by Eric Berne (1964) and "I'm Ok – You're OK" by Thomas Harris (1967).

The rapport mentioned above represents a blatant stunting of our emotional growth largely due to factors connected to formation of our *shadow* coupled with the desire to absolve ourselves of being *accountable* (visa vi' being blamed) for the situations we find ourselves in. The hardest part of recognizing that *accountability* is necessary for our autonomy is that we must first accept the fact that it is our own decisions that have delivered us to our current situations. Once we have integrated *acceptance* and *accountability* into our life approach, we must then be constantly on guard to prevent defensive mechanisms from taking charge in our experiencing.

If we are to have any goals relative to our personal growth, they should only be comprised of an effort to "clear" ourselves of any motives toward acquiring circumstances that will contribute to our building an emotional nest preventing us from encountering the world as it is instead of being only compliant with our preferences, thereby, strengthening our tendency toward preventing the unfolding of our awareness. Any effort toward "building something" must be observed with a fine eye toward ferreting out any motivation focused toward acquiring a sense of permanence in our earthly journey. In this, we must realize that whatever we attempt to "hold and control," in the larger scheme of things, eventually becomes that which "holds and controls" us, thereby, becoming an obstacle to "clearing" our *shadow*. Even though it is believed that "ignorance is bliss," it still leaves us with a nagging feeling that there will always be something or someone in our environment with the potential to undermine our "security." Alan Watts (1951) addressed this superbly by stating that, "The only security there is, is knowing that there is none."

So awareness is our third step reflecting a constant vigil toward allowing the resurfacing and the reintegrating of our *shadow* through disarming and sanctioning its defense mechanisms. To understand the tenacity, cleverness and innovativeness of our *ego* and the necessity for the constancy of our vigil, one only has to imagine a hungry fox outside a chicken coup and his single minded and relentless desire to sate his hunger.

In our next step is where we begin to select an endeavor in which to apply our energy which has not yet been subject to the effects of *toxic shame*. If an individual has experienced an upbringing with a "blanket" toxic assault to his self-concept, this may be more difficult than what one might suppose. Selecting a direction for the energy application must be contemplated with great care.

THE FOURTH STEP: VISION

So far we have put our energy into creating a "clear field" in which to operate. The question next posed is what are we clearing the field for? However, before we cover the perception of *vision* and its utility, it is necessary to understand an important distinction between *ego* and *Ego*.

The little *ego* builds structures in order to have a more tangible representation for perceiving a more detailed and clearly defined sense of self. The big *Ego* clears outdated structure in order to be unobstructed for receiving the *intuition* that presents the vision without the "tarnishing" side issues that the self may add in the form of *shadow* and its attendant defense mechanisms. Even though our emphasis is on working with *Ego*, *both* perspectives are needed: *ego* provides the worldly tools and *Ego* provides the focus. The *ego* is the "do" and the *Ego* is the direction. Our culture is so overly investing in "doing something" and to where we are seen as a person "making a difference" that we have lost sight of the complete overall *vision* that occurs when we are free of personal and practical motives. In this instance the master craftsman has allowed his tools to dictate the focus of his creation. In these steps we must be more concerned with getting a clearer understanding of how we may understand the process of "returning" to Eden, or the undoing of what we have set in motion out of fear, anger, desire and ambition through the assumption that our "doing something" about these feelings will, magically, alleviate our feeling of emptiness. In truth, our programmed reactions, conscious and unconscious, only serve to intensify our feelings of frustration by giving them practical expression. The *vision* we receive through our *intuition* is an expression of what our life could potentially be if we were free of our *ego's* motives. It is for this reason that we want to take action as a result of inner focus rather than that of external "need."

Our *vision* is a creative projection of what our *intuition* tells us that there is a void in the world for. It's almost as if each individual's creative projection "fills a gap" or completes a picture that the world's energy may flow more smoothly and inclusively of every individual who participates in it. It should not be confused with what might be considered a problem solving perspective comprised of compensatory factors. There are, truly, creative ways of handling world problems but *vision* is much more concerned with the openness of expression rather than with the functionality of application.

Feelings of creativity and openness of expression are factors that contribute tremendously to the development of a solid and comfortable self concept. How an individual's expression is met by the world, especially by their early caretakers, speaks volumes about their attitudes toward and confidence in participating in future worldly endeavors. An individual's upbringing must develop with a delicate balance between worldly acknowledgement, encouragement and acceptance and the individual's experience with healthy shame. We must have influences that catalyze our expression yet apprise us of "reasonable" human limits. Over emphasized shame leads to toxicity and unwarranted recognition and excessive patronization leads to narcissism. If a parent or caretaker has been raised without this balance, they will be unaware of the delicacy needed let alone the insight required to contribute to it. Unfortunately, this assumption reflects the bulk of our civilization. Although the balance may be absent in the caretaker(s), one may still argue that this absence produces a social environment leading to self awareness in the caretaker through the reflected behaviors of their offspring. If one held a belief in intelligent design, this potential would certainly hold merit through an assumed deific intent. It should also be noted that both religion *and* metaphysics assume intelligent design though different in their application.

So, where does this leave us in selecting a *vision* to "feed?" Perhaps developing an analogous scenario would render a theme to explore our choices. To accomplish this we need to establish a history for our young person George. Although George has a fairly vivid memory dating back to about one and a half, his self-concept issue began to take solid form around the age of four. George's upbringing most decidedly was of the type who's *Beta Point* was often fixed at the far left on our graph residing in the *toxic shame* domain. Fear was the dominant emotion. Any attempt to establish a sense of autonomy was rapidly and severely extinguished through his interactions with his caretakers. When George attempted to voice his opinions and feeling about his experiences and interactions with them, his father melted into the environment and his mother, who had her own issues emanating from a diminished self-concept (compensatory narcissism), invalidated George's expressions by emphasizing that everyone else in the world had "been there and done that" (meaning that she had) and that what he felt and thought were nothing new. His originality was never even considered let alone acknowledged. George had a reasonable amount of chores assigned relative to his changing age, however, the completion of every task drew criticism with the recognition of any work well done going virtually unrecognized. All George's discoveries and victories were invalidated through diminishment or the absence of encouragement. His mother enhanced positive feelings about herself through diminishing others. His father had retreated into passive aggression. George's spirit, as the horse in the previous sections, had been completely broken and he lived with only two emotions: fear and anger,

anger being a derivative of fear. Anger became his only weapon of defense feeding rebellion. His safest and easiest path to emotional and physical safety was to withdraw into self imposed isolation through hiding.

There were many other causes for the *toxic shame* that George felt. Yet, depending on the current generation and its trends, the contributions encountered, by George's generation and others, will vary. The latest and most popular current child rearing contributors are ignoring (abandonment) and neglect. The effects exhibit as rage and projected entitlement (compensatory narcissism). Every generation has a major compliment of children attempting to survive and extricate their self-concept from the feelings associated with *toxic shame*. This process often takes a lifetime. Generally, the contemporary contributing causes reside on the subconscious and unconscious levels of both child and caretaker and are reciprocally reflective of contemporary desires and fads. To the "objective" observer these needs and desires can easily be seen underlying current advertising objectives. Generational desires coupled with Adler's inevitable *inferiority complex* (Adler, 1927) compose a formidable psychological composite that must be worked through, understood and overcome by every generation. For many, success never occurs and they remain unable to achieve "adult status" failing to shed their roll as a parent or a child as structured by *Transactional Analysis* (Berne, 1964).

So the task for George seems monumental with, what appears to be, no way around. However, if George could find an endeavor(s) that his caretakers had neither knowledge of nor experience in, and having done so, keep it a secret for as long as he was able, he could slowly forge an autonomous skill(s) in it and the barrier against his self-realization would slowly begin to crack. Family businesses and children who opt for similar careers to their families are rife with emotionally neurotic interdependencies and *toxic shame* passed down generation to generation through the perpetuation of their perceived inadequacies and the child rearing practices formed by them. Repair of the child's self-concept often begins when the children escapes the diminishing affects of their caretakers, for example, when the child opts to go into the art field when their caretakers are accountants or go into philosophy when the caretakers are heavily into business. The opposite might also occur when the parents are involved in philosophy and art and the child opts for business or science. The key to initiating repair is to select an area of endeavor or field that allows breathing space apart from the mindset and environment that is familiar to his caretakers. In the new field the caretakers have no means of comparison to perpetuate the shaming. Their only remaining means of assault would be a personally direct assault on the child's character for selecting a field that is different from theirs and that they have no knowledge or respect for. In many cases, for example, where the child has an excelling talent for business and accounting, similar to their caretakers, but the caretakers' child rearing practices have set the youth in rebellion against their wishes and methods, it deprives him of an endeavor that he may have been eminently successful in had he instead had approval and encouragement from his caretakers. Essentially, a career potential has been eliminated due to self-concept issues originated by the caretakers. These rebellious urges become well integrated with the child's defense mechanisms and obscure any clarity that could be had toward the child's successful self-realization. He will then spend the rest of his life looking for encouragement and attempting to overcome his fear of taking autonomous and confident action in the field of his choice never understanding the dynamics that inhibit him.

Again, there are many more trained reactions to the environment that contributes to inhibiting George's ability to overcome the blanketing inertia that his *toxic shaming* has produced. No one factor is a "cure-all" for self-concept repair. There is no "magic pill." However, selecting an endeavor as far apart as possible from the focus of his caretakers is a major step on the road to autonomy and self-realization.

Having ignored the intensity of the mind chatter, the *ego* and its focus on its believed and fabricated needs, and then amplifying our attention toward the direction provided by the *Ego*, we can now formulate how we would like to express our choices in ways that would draw the least amount of interference from those who have a vested interest in how we choose to act whether to maintain the cloaking of *their shadow* or to advance the implementation of *their* perceived desires and needs. In the quietude, the subtle voice of our *intuition* sends us fully formed *visions* of how our choices might "play out" in life's theatre. The path of least resistance is usually the most "in line" with how the universal energy would most likely flow. Perceiving this factor occurs through the fifth step; *Potential*.

THE FIFTH STEP: POTENTIAL

After we have selected a *vision* to invest in and the energy begins to flow in the direction that we have selected, we often find individuals who encourage and catalyze our dreams in the form of mentors and peers. Our intuition tells us who can be "trusted" not to manipulate us for the preservation of their personal *shadow*. Our intuition, when we're paying attention, tells us the area that we may invest our energies unhampered through giving us "flashes" of completed possible experiences.

An important and necessary understanding to be had is that *we must be in action* in order to receive a response from the universe to our chosen direction. It is the response that we receive from our environment that tells us of the potential that can be anticipated within a possible experience. However, it is all too often that we choose an action and wait for a response to our choice from the universe and our surrounding environment. If there is no action, there will be no response. Remember, the material world operates on the principle of polarity. If we don't take specific action in a particular direction, no "opposite and equal" action will be returned. Yet, knowing this, we still hesitate to move at a crossroads even after we have made a choice. Even in light of a difficult choice, a principle rendered by the practice of Zen says that if we are faced with two options of equal merit and that neither reveals enough emphasis to elicit a "definitive" choice, begin taking action on either one and our heart will immediately react with which choice "feels right" for us. Remember, evidence processing is a function of the mind and polarity driven. *Intuition*, which is *always* right, is a function of our inner awareness. The question then arises, are we listening?

Even in light of the fact that the universe follows the path of least resistance, we often select a path that seems to be overloaded with it. The resistance perceived may not actually indicate that the path chosen would be ill advised simply by virtue of its resistance. There are other factors which may mitigate our assessment of choice. Oddly enough, there are two variations of resistance that must be explored to properly assess a selection. One possibility for response is dependent on environmental factors and the other is dependent on personal attachment coupled with *shadow* defense mechanisms. Our discrimination between the two must be honest and must be, essentially, brutal as related to our feelings.

The first variation of resistance we may encounter simply emanates from environmental circumstances. If the direction we have selected for the investment of our energy and efforts includes many other individuals with the same focus and intention, their combined influence may have already created a surge of energy that, according to the natural dynamic of the law of attraction, is already in process creating the corresponding "equal and opposite force" that we encounter even before we had applied *our* energy to it. In this case it may be a bit more difficult to "see" the environment's response to our choice cleanly and as a solitary response to our individual efforts. The environmental response is mingled with that of others who are also on the same path. For example, we might have selected a specific branch of art to invest our efforts in. We know the art to be substantially different in life focus than that of our caretakers who are both immersed in business and are unfamiliar with the trappings of an art experience. However, it may be such that there are many others involved in the type of art expression we have chosen and have incurred opposition from others in the art field who disagree with the approach of our selected branch. We may, perhaps, be more invested in impressionism, while others in the field place more value on realism, and, hence, we feel the environmental resistance to our choice *within* the field. We must be careful not to interpret this environmental response as an indicator that this is not the field where we should invest our efforts due to the resistance we encounter. In this we must listen more deeply to our *intuition* for more decisive indicators relative to whom and what are actually responsible for the resistance we feel. Unfortunately, we may also attract peers and superiors in the field with the same approach to social interaction as had our caretakers due to the natural law of attraction drawing to us those of identical or opposite resonance. However, without the personal emotional connections to and faith we had placed in our caretakers throughout our upbringing, there will be much less of a coercive and demeaning effect by virtue of the fact that new experiences will be "outside" of or "once removed" from our original emotional "investment" in experiences with our caretakers. This understanding confirms why it is easier to change or adjust our patterns and behaviors with "strangers" than with our families. "Strangers" most certainly have less expectation of us than our families and caretakers.

The first variation of resistance is relatively easy to "see" since it involves responses easily discriminated from the "outside" world. The second variation, however, is much more convoluted in that it not only has the interplay with the "outside" world but also includes the deviousness of our rationalizing mind with heavy investments in defense mechanisms due to its involvement with *toxic shame* and its partnership with the *ego*.

There are four levels of *defense mechanisms* (Vaillant, 1992). In response to shame they vary in their intensity depending on the depth and extent of shame conditioning. *Toxic shame* will produce the most *pathological* defense and *healthy shame* will produce the most *mature*. The two middle levels are *immature* and *neurotic*, respectively, and are the most common problematic defenses. These two levels include *projection, intellectualization, reaction formation, dissociation, displacement and repression* which easily lend themselves toward the principle of polarity. Perhaps it would be best to handle the explanation of the second variation with examples and then delineate them.

Let's first look at Timothy and his use of *projection*. Timothy's father is a driven executive who is highly competitive. He is demanding and rarely offers compliment except for exceptional work. His mother could be considered a "trophy wife." She is vain and requires high maintenance and due to her looks has never had to develop skills other than social navigation. She expects Timothy to cater to her and then disappear when catering is not needed. As Timothy grew up his father was more demanding of him than of his employees. He was highly critical and intolerant, and still is, of mediocre and poor performance. His driven temperament has broken Timothy's spirit (remember the horse from a previous section) driving him far into *toxic shame* by instilling an overwhelming sense of fear and inadequacy. Physical beatings for transgressions dominated his earlier years reinforcing the fear aspect. He is now in his thirties and has had difficulty maintaining employment and choosing a career. He has recently acquired a job in the "white collar" sector and is having difficulty dealing with his immediate boss who, in many respects, is like his father. Timothy has a gnawing, nebulous feeling of inadequacy; however, the feeling has not yet surfaced into his consciousness. He is unable to keep up with the demands of his work environment and is sliding further and further behind. His perspective is that if anything can go wrong it will and that his boss delegates his own work to him and others (safety in numbers) because he is incompetent in doing it himself. His *ego* has saved face through compensating for his felt inadequacies by holding the perspective that he is doing the work of someone who supposedly is more skilled and of a higher position than he by choosing to believe that he is doing more than is required of him and that he is working above and beyond the duties of his job description. The *projection* of his perceived inadequacies provides him with a positive self-concept and justification for failing at the same time. Convincing himself that he is doing more than is required of him also allows him to choose not to apply more effort, thereby, preventing any risk of future failure. In this scenario, his *ego* is in control and he has effectively, if only temporarily, *shadowed* his *toxically shamed* feeling of inadequacy through the defense mechanism of *projection*.

Diane has opted for *reaction formation* to be her best defense. Her environment includes a very strict and domineering mother and a father who is passively aggressive and a philanderer. Her mother is very rigid in her religious beliefs contending that sexual activities should be limited only to procreation and that pleasure seeking is a perversion of our earthly journey. Due to her mother's perspective on sex and pleasure, her father has had to resort to finding his enjoyment elsewhere while becoming evasive and sarcastic as a product of being driven "underground" by Diane's mother. Though her father may have been able to "slip away,"

Diane has been left to feel the full brunt of the shame inducing effects of her mother's over bearing religious perspective prohibiting and punishing for her emotional and physical expression for anything other than religious reasons. Like Timothy, whose *toxic shaming* focused on an assigned incompetence, Diane's *toxic shaming* also broke her spirit but through shaming her natural urges.

As children grow and as our culture dogmatically instills a mostly inconscious division between the sexes through stereotypically treating each differently, they learn how to adapt to these differences through the role modeling of their parents. Early on there are virtually no other perspectives for choice offered for example leaving their parents as the prevailing examples of differentiation dominating over their outer world exposure. The children know nothing other than what they see in their immediate family. As they become more aware of their own sex they arrive at having to choose which behaviors to follow toward their own aspirations. However, when there is a conflict between their models and their own temperament mixes badly with their same sexed parent, they face a serious dilemma. Not wanting to lose their budding fragile identity or the affection of either parent, they must seek a way to resolve the conflict within themselves.

As Diane moved into puberty, she slowly became aware that her own sensuality and feeling for sex were much the same as the temperament of her father. Her mother's suppression of any discussions about sex and its peripheral issues in her family only served to polarize the issue within her more. Anything related to sex or sensuality was vehemently attacked by her mother while her father remained quiet. In addition to suppression, her mother indirectly levied accusations against the father in a third person fashion where it left no doubt in Diane's mind that it was her father she was talking about. Early on Diane was daddy's little girl but over time her mother's relentless vigilance and exaggerated punishments for what she considered perverse expression crossed Diane's *Beta Point* into *toxic shame* and Diane slowly withdrew her affections for her father as a result of her mother's overwhelming onslaught. The fact that her mother was the dominating influence and that her father had receded into the shadows left Diane no alternative but to align herself with the power in order to maintain her position and survival in the family. Her affinity for sex and the love for her father had to be integrated into her persona so that they would not interfere with the image of her developing *ego*. The intensity of the shaming by her mother was so replete that she opted to become a nun. There she could deny her "flaws of character" by staunchly advocating them as "human frailties" which must be overcome (*reaction formation*). This way she could see herself as answering her guilt and "doing penance to become pure." In this light she could give her dad love and affection she wanted by seeing him as a "poor sinner" requiring compassion and mercy. As she took on the garb and the persona of her religion she grew in passion and intensity against any of the sexual or sensual urges that came up within her as the "work of the devil" (*displacement*). By "giving it to God" and blaming the "devil" she could also absolve herself of being responsible for them. In this scenario, her *ego* is in control and she has effectively, if only temporarily, *shadowed* her *toxically shamed* feelings of unworthiness through the defense mechanism of *reaction formation* (becoming a nun) and *displacement* (the "devil" is responsible for her urges).

The mind most certainly has the ability and deviousness to be able to twist the logic of self-perception in a way where an individual may view himself more favorably despite their actual "appearance" to others. It is important to note that which defense mechanism is chosen says a lot about the person's implementation of their chosen *locus of control*. *Reaction formation* applies the adapted perspective to the self and *projection* and *displacement* applies the adaptation to others. Perhaps more understanding and research is needed relative to the perspective Vaillant uses in the ordering of defense mechanisms into pathological, immature, neurotic and mature levels (Vaillant, 1992).

So, as we come back to our discussion about our variations of resistance in the responses that we receive from the "outer world" and our inner selves, we can see that it is extremely important to become clear about our choices by digging as deeply as we can into our motivation and recognizing where the resistance may be coming from and assessing it properly relative to selecting careers or activities that are free of *toxic shaming* aspects derived from our early experiences. Both Timothy and Diane were unable to see past their defenses until much later in life when they encountered other experiences, free of the *toxic shaming* mechanism, building the confidence in themselves enough to accept themselves as they were rather than who they were supposed to be. In this we can see the tremendous power contained in the selection of our dominating *locus of control*.

The fifth step, *Potential*, provides us a response from the universe and our inner self to our chosen endeavor so that we may assess the type of resistance connected to our choices. As long as the resistance is not of our own making, we have the potential for the success in our chosen endeavor toward yielding positive reinforcement that will contributing to an improved self-concept, thereby, diminishing the effects of our previous *toxic shaming* through a slow attrition.

THE SIXTH STEP: MOTIVATION

Once we've decided on a goal, it then becomes necessary to "begin production." We've gone through the test model by taking enough action for the universal energy to react and have then assessed our potential for success. We must now create "movement" in the chosen direction accepting the resistance perceived thus far as "what comes with the territory." The task is to develop momentum enough to carry and power our endeavors. This comes in the form of what most people call *motivation*.

Our *motivation* comes in two forms: *incitement* and *application*. *Incitement* is essentially the trigger that catches our attention, encourages us and directs us toward materializing an endeavor. This form is the easiest to contend with provided there are no other endeavors or concerns absorbing our time and energy while distracting or preventing us from being aware of available opportunities. *Application* relates to the applying of energy for the purpose of overcoming inertia, inertia being the tendency for objects to remain moving or not until acted upon by an external force. Simply put, we must apply enough "push" in order to "get the ball rolling" so it moves under its own power and momentum. This is most certainly easier said than done.

In the social sciences we can consider inertia as our tendency to maintain our learned behavior patterning in relation to the people and situations in the surrounding environment. All animals, including humans, are reluctant to change a conditioned (learned) pattern of behavior, even in light of the fact that the change may make their survival easier. Usually, our comfort rests in our sense of security. Our security is a function of a maintained and consistent feeling of safety. Remember, natural law always works toward returning to a balance or quality of rest through the process of entropy.

For us to expend the effort to overcome inertia we must believe that there is a viable reason to do so and that it will, ultimately, benefit our sense of security and feeling of well being. For the individual who has been the recipient of *toxic shaming*, this is all the more imperative. Those *toxically shamed* are much less likely to risk change than those who haven't as they have been taught that when they extend themselves they are almost always "assassinated" with a demeaning response from their environment. Even if the environmental response is essentially innocent, they rationalize a way to perceive it as a threat thereby giving them permission not to risk. We often hear a verbal representation of this from the general population when we hear someone blaming "Murphy's Law" for their mishap or failure stating that if something *can* go wrong it will.

Even in lieu of "Murphy's Law" we can see how the selection of an endeavor to invest in is best taken from experiences that have received the least amount of shaming, visa vi, an area of life that previous caretakers and current shamers have very little, if any, experience in dealing with. That being said, let's look at some of the avenues through which we might build internal *motivation* and momentum.

Self-Talk – Often times, even if we haven't done it ourselves, we hear people talking to themselves as if someone were speaking encouraging words to them for the actions that they are currently taking. It may take the form of a prepared dialogue or an ad lib conversation with a part of themselves that would like to accomplish a particular task. This may also take the form of what the contemporary metaphysical community calls an affirmation. The principle inference is that if we say something enough times we will, first, start to believe it and then, second, create enough momentum in the application of energy and intention to draw an experience that will make the thought a self fulfilling prophesy. This is the basis for the currently held perspective of the Law of Attraction. It has merit due to the fact that sounds and words, have a vibratory power in themselves and will produce a manifestation through attracting like vibrations to themselves.

Emulation and Identity – If we look at successful people who are either in the career we've chosen to pursue or have been successful at an endeavor we have chosen to invest in, we will tend to find personal traits that resonate with ours and allow ourselves to speculate that if they could be successful, so could we. In a more complete investigation, many of us may read the biographies of notable people in our field in order to "stack the deck" with more specific information contributing toward the building a believable *vision* that we may have confidence in pursuing. In observing and reading about similar personalities, life styles and experiences of those who are successful and through feeling a similarity with them we are able to allow ourselves to get closer to believing that we have the same potential. This action seems to temporarily suspend the effects of some of the *toxically shamed* qualities residing in our *shadow* allowing us to develop hope for attaining personal worth. On a commensurate path, we can also see emulating a biographical path as an alternate way of regaining more of an *internal locus of control.*

Having a Sponsor or a Model – One step closer than having a biographical example to read about is having a successful personal sponsor or advisor to "feel into" or to ask questions directly of giving us an understanding of what it takes to be successful and confident in fuller dimension. A book can only impart so much as compared to a live person who provides a better "rounded" example. In addition to the possibility of more compete model, the sponsor or advisor will also provide encouragement thereby diminishing the effects of *toxic shame* even further. As an important note here, it is important to be cautious of the defense mechanism, *projection*, as we may attribute positive qualities in ourselves to our sponsor or model in an effort not to have to fulfill the potential of those qualities within ourselves and thereby avoid changing our inertial emotional patterns to accommodate them.

Invest in Research on the Subject – To a lesser degree, at least initially; our own curiosity in a subject may spur a quest for information and understanding if only to fulfill a hunger for awareness about something that has been sparked in our interest. Whether a rekindled interest from a past life or simply through someone who we had respect for that drew our attention in a particular direction, something resonated within us that drew us in that direction. This usually only occurs if we, at the least, have a passing attentiveness to our own *intuitive* voice.

Find Like Minded Individuals – In lieu of having a sponsor we may also seek out individuals with similar interests, if not for the social component, which is a very strong draw, but simply for the information that would be available to us simply by asking of those who we have befriended. One word of caution, however. Even though we may attract those of a similar interest, we may also attract those of similar limitation. This may produce a feeling of "safety in numbers" insulating us from exerting risk by virtue of perceived group *toxic shame*. It is imperative that our Third Step of *Awareness* must be fully in play in order that we may see through any group rationalizations leading to self deception.

All these methods have the effect of minimizing the paralyzing "inaction" of inertia. After all, the word motive comes from the Latin *motivere* meaning to move. We may employ one or any combination of methods. We can do this consciously or unconsciously. For some it occurs through the instinct that comes as the result of past training.

At this point I need to emphasize the power behind simple focus. That is, *choosing* to think about things that will assist in our motivation. I cannot stress enough the devastating effects of focusing on what is *not believed to be possible* as a cloaked encouragement toward inertia by the part of us that is *toxically shamed*. It will take time and effort to train ourselves to continually, over and over, refocus back on subjects that will expand our effectiveness rather than focusing on what we have been unable to do in the past due to the paralyzing effects of our toxic conditioning. Energy follows thought. Remember, to focus on our enemy, all the reasons we have learned why we *can't* do something, gives it power over us. Remember that belief is still a choice as a result of personal experience. Through our new motivation we are slowly forging a new experience that will allow us to put our self-concept in a better light through our renewed focus on positive and constructive endeavors free of the limiting effects of our past conditioning.

At this point it's important to note that maintaining motivation for an, as yet, unknown experience could be considered distressing at best. In this day and age of instant everything, the expectation for returns on whatever we put our energy into is as short as instant oatmeal. As part of the western culture we tend to lose interest and become discouraged easily. Coupled with our expectation of speed, we compound the frustrating effects by adding the problem of *toxic shaming*. The individual who is shamed will tend to search for other areas of life and activities for which their shaming caretakers may show approval. It's much like a child rummaging through a box surfacing items as fast as they can, waiting for the approving nod of the caretaker when the proper item or activity is found. When the nod doesn't come, the rummager becomes faster and faster almost to the point of desperation. Any semblance of learned patience becomes a cold memory. Approval almost never comes. As our rummager grows older, the searching expands to include work and career choices. How deeply and how long our individual remains working at a career depends on how intense the *toxic shaming* was. The more shame, the less confidence, the shorter they stay with what doesn't produce approval. We have to begin to wonder if today's "job hopping" tendencies are simply a function of our growing financial hard times and our survival or are there much deeper issues at play?

Building and maintaining the energy for motivation is very much like training a small child who has differing intentions. After a number of times of being redirected toward a direction more to our liking, the child's urge to persist will diminish and the energy in the new direction will build and take precedence. In the child as well as an adult, an old urge or habit will eventually die of attrition taking with it its paired toxic programming leaving the new habit to grow in the void with our applied focus. We know that when we make a big deal of what, in our eyes, a child is doing wrong, they tend to blown it out of proportion attempting to absorb the maximum amount of energy and attention. We meet much less stress and energy loss by ignoring what is the *least* desirable and focusing on what is the *most* desirable. If you don't believe me try it, not only on children, but on adults as well. After all, aren't we just big children with social polishing? This approach is just the opposite perspective of using our Chinese axiom "to acknowledge your enemy gives them power." I guess we might call it "reverse philosophy."

The important concept to emphasize here is the need for a consistent reinforcing of whatever motivational method(s) we have chose to do the "ramping up" of our chosen activity. It is here where the potential to overcome inertia must be generated, at the least, until the energy producing the new endeavor tips the scales against what is used to maintain inertia.

So the Sixth Step is concerned with inciting and maintaining *motivation* toward an endeavor free of prior negative conditioning. Free of attachments and judgments, our self-concept is free to blossom and grow in a direction that is healthy and encouraging.

THE SEVENTH STEP: CHANGE

The seventh step, *change*, sounds much easier than it actually is. As we garner motivation, we must now also apply the energy toward taking action. Everything up to this point, except for our trial runs, has been primarily preparation for beginning an endeavor with the intention of replacing old behaviors connected to *toxic shaming*. This would be equivalent to applying for and actually performing a job solicited or engaging in a hobby or activity that *motivation* was incited and maintained for.

The reason that I say that it sounds easier than we might think is because one of the most detracting factors tending to short circuit the flow of what might be considered by the *ego* as risky new activity is *procrastination*. We might even consider it a "mature" type of a defense mechanism. However, this is not simply the type that puts things off but the posing of logical and socially acceptable reasons for postponing the activity with the unspoken awareness of others knowing that it truly is not a totally honest or valid reason while allowing it to pass as so. These reasons include "not being ready," excessive preparation of the space or tools for the activity and other socially acceptable "obligations" that might take precedence over the new activity. We know that these reasons are simply excuses permitting one not to invest in an activity that might, from the perspective of the *ego*, potentially result in more shaming or an exposure of perceived unworthiness. The *ego* is extremely clever and can always find a way to protect itself from loss of control and image; real or imagined. Ultimately, we're not trying to injure the *ego,* but merely "doing an end run around it," in an attempt to redirect the activity toward being out of the reach of its familiar sphere of control.

Through the actual *change* is where we will accumulate the positive responses that will empower a sense of worthiness through a growing set of repeated experiences that are free of past conditioned diminishing. As those experiences increase in number, they will eventually "push out" the conditioned shameful feelings and replace them with feelings of positive rapport and confidence in dealing with the world contributing toward building a positive self-concept. Remember, it's our experience that validates and justifies the beliefs we choose for ourselves. The laws governing energy and creation are such that whatever we apply energy and attention to grows in effect and dominance much like feeding a plant with water and food. If we apply compromised water and food (like shaming mechanisms), the plant will grow in a dysfunctional fashion adapting to the effects of the contamination. If we apply clean water and health inducing food, the plant will grow unfettered and according to its natural molecular blueprint. In this respect, we are no different than the plant.

It is important to know that what we have selected as an objective must NOT be a reaction to the people and circumstances we have encountered along the way. Our direction must be solidly rooted in what our *Ego*, or inner *intuition*, has directed us toward. In itself, this is a pure rendition of our creativity as an individual. We may look to others for assistance in applying techniques that will clarify our project but the conceptual focus must remain of our own making. By allowing our *intuition* to direct our focus, it will allow us to develop the talents that are specific to us as individuals. This in turn will give us a very solid sense of self. With the accent on individual talent rather than a competitive comparison, we can build a strong self-concept based on our individual efforts and experience rather that the opinions and ulterior motives of other shame inducing individuals.

Rebuilding a strong self-concept is largely the result of accumulating encouraging experiences that support our newly chosen endeavors. As the number of positive responses from the universe increases, the more confident the self-concept becomes. It occurs much like moving water, beginning with ripples in the "egoic landscape" and as experiences accumulate, small waves begin to emerge. As their effects progressively multiply and spread throughout the landscape, the movement become "tsunamic" in nature as long as we continue to move *with* the flow. The beginning of this growth is difficult at best, as it is with any emerging seedling. Early on we are still dealing with some of the self talk that was generated by early toxic conditioning composed of self doubt, discouraging and intimidating childhood discussions and the initial fears that are inherent in any new experience generated by the knowledge that self growth must always lead to change which threatens the *ego's* sense of control and security. It is for this reason that the *ego* doesn't always see increased competency as a positive result. If we can, instead, perceive fear as excitement, we can bypass much of our trepidation. Fear and excitement have much the same effect on the body and emotions. They differ only in our choice as to whether we approach or avoid the experience.

Another important result of our growing self confidence is that it begins a slow shift in our dominant *locus of control* from external toward operating more from an internal perspective. If we remember, external *locus of control* is the belief or assumption that external factors have more of an effect on our world than our personal will and choices. Positive responses and encouragement from the world gives us more of a sense of personal power making our *locus of control* much more internal. This, essentially, produces a shift in our *Beta Point* through increasing the effectiveness of our internally motivated actions. However, we must also remember that too strong an internal *locus of control* produces just as many issues as one that is too weak. Essentially, we are endeavoring to create a balance between the two if we are to realize the true sense of compassion without the compensatory influences of an overly dominant internally or externally generated *locus of control*.

Rebuilding our self-concept is a slow and gradual process requiring patience and tenacity. These are qualities which have become much scarcer as a result of our encroaching tendencies and beliefs concerning instant gratification. The current western tendency where our young exhibit such a sense of entitlement is a direct reflection of the *toxic shame* and *narcissism* conflict inherent in living in such a competitive and self oriented environment. The slowly growing disappearance of learned manners only serves to expose this effect more starkly.

Balancing all these conflicting influences is much like walking on the edge of a razor. Submitting to any of the "breezes" of past conditioning can knock us off our path into the chasms of compensation on either side if we are not paying attention. The key to our balance is our diligence at maintaining a continual sense of awareness at all times. This requires a tremendous amount of energy and effort and why the mastery of the self is such a prized possession.

THE EIGHTH STEP: BALANCE

In all climbing toward accomplishment, there are "plateaus." This is one of them. Here we rest and reassess our efforts thus far. This is sometimes difficult, especially, for the westerner as we are all used to "doing something" as opposed to simply observing by stepping back from action. When we are in action we are, usually, not perceiving the surrounding circumstances by virtue of being occupied with our immediate efforts. Stepping back is necessary and extremely important if we are to gain a reasonably "objective" assessment of how we have performed thus far. Our assessing will primarily be focused on searching for ulterior motives connected to the *ego* that may have "slipped by" while we were focused on garnering the necessary energy to increase our motivation toward our new, "toxic" free endeavors.

It is at this time that we judge whether the reasons for acting and the types of motivations chosen were actually the best match or fit for the experience(s) we had. Did they solicit negative reinforcement? Did we take into account the difference between the feedback we received from the natural universe rather than from those whose "support" of and participation with us were underpinned with encouragement toward our obligation to them induced through guilt or shame? Essentially, were we used by others? Did the results we obtained actually make us feel better about ourselves? Did our results give us a reason to feel proud? Did our results highlight a proficiency or sense of accomplishment within us? Our assessment must include every angle of perception we are able to conceive of. It's important that we leave no stone unturned so that we have total faith in that the action we performed and the results we perceived are free of any self-diminishing factors. Our utmost honesty is imperative if we are to accept the positive image of ourselves that this toxic free activity brings to us. There must be no room for doubt as to the validity of what we have done. The *last* thing we want to do is tell ourselves something about ourselves that we cannot honestly prove to ourselves. In this situation, rationalization is our arch-enemy. This assessment *MUST* be of our own generation. The opinion of others is *not valid* in this case. It's what got us into trouble in the first place – believing the opinions of others about our self-worth. Even if the opinion comes from someone whom we implicitly trust, it is not applicable. It is still hear say and subject to our personal doubt and the potential for a change in the opinions of others. The assessment *MUST* come from our own experience and values. The point of assessing with such strict guidelines is that we are forging a new component of our self-concept which must be totally beyond the potential for self reproach or doubt.

When our assessment is painfully honest, it gives us a clear indication as to what parts of our experience are in accord with our best interests and what aspects are off relative to our objectives. Then, it just becomes a matter of adjusting our *motivation* and *application* in the right direction. Usually, small changes are all that are necessary to bring the responses more in line with what we are looking for. As we gather more positive results, we build an escrow of validated self-worth. This allows us to become less invested in responses and more invested in our curiosity and interests. This is essentially, a shift from an external to more of an internal *locus of control* as directed by our *Ego*.

THE STEPS IN A NUTSHELL

The whole purpose of the eight steps is to replace a history of negative, discouraging experiences with a new set of positive encouraging ones by simply focusing on what we want rather than what we feel a lack of. Remember that focusing on what we don't want; essentially, reproduces the attitudes and circumstances that allow them to occur. Since energy follows attention, focusing on what we do want serves to feed our new endeavors while allowing the old discouraging experiences to die of attrition. This has the effect of gradually *reframing* our attitude and approach toward how we live our lives through the growing positive responses to our chosen "toxic free" projects and endeavors. With this thought in mind, let's review the steps more concisely in a summary.

The *acceptance* of the *First Step* simply refers to receiving and accepting whatever the world presents to us as it is presented. That includes whether we receive a person, circumstance, experience or material possession or loss. In doing this we must have a sense of consistency. That is, this attitude must be present *all the time*. We don't need to "do" anything, just openly receive what comes into our sphere of influence. Let it occur. Granted, there may be situations where there is a risk to someone's life. In this we should attempt to prevent harm to a person or animal. Other than that, like Paul McCartney says, "Let it Be."

The *accountability* of the *Second Step* refers to taking ownership for any choices that may have put us in a situation; pleasurable or not. For example, if we are caught in a riot, it didn't just "happen" to us. We made a series of choices that led us to being in the proximity of or even involved in a riotous experience through the feeling that we projected; whether of victim or perpetrator. For many individuals the excuse tendered is "sh*!^t happens." In quoting this they are implying that the cause came strictly from the "outside" of their influence or control. They have rationalized that they have no responsibility for their involvement. Remember, however, that there is also the saying that says "it takes two" reminding us that nothing ever just "happens to us." We are always responsible for our choices. My contention is that we are partly responsible for *every* situation we contact or find ourselves involved in simply by virtue of what we do or don't do to attract it to us.

The *awareness* of the *Third Step* involves three parts. The first part is that that awareness must continually be in place for discovering and "routing out" our *shadows* and reintegrating those "unacceptable" aspects of our personality and character back into conscious acceptance. While unconscious, they remain a powerful and invisible threat through subconscious coercion limiting growth through new experiences. The second part of being aware is recognizing when our *defense mechanisms* are in play defending the remaining implanted *shadows* that protect the *ego*. The last part is when picking new endeavors to invest in that they are free from of any connections to *toxically shaming* influences.

The *vision* of the *Fourth Step* involves the selecting of an endeavor, or perhaps a career, where we can see ourselves being creative and productive in an area of life that our caretakers or shame producing influences have little or no experience in leaving us free to invest ourselves without the coercive and interfering effects of *toxic shame* and *shadow*. With no preconception or assumption of inadequacy, we can freely invest our time and energy in an endeavor while allowing room for the potential of building self confidence and autonomy. This is where we take our first steps in a new direction.

The *potential* of the *Fifth Step* is where we take our first action toward our selected endeavor(s) and patiently wait for the universe to respond. We then assess the responses that we receive as either encouragement or resistance. We, obviously, welcome encouragement, however, with every investment of energy there is always an element of resistance. Our potential for success is decided upon, not only on received encouragement, but on the type of resistance we receive. As we separate out our perception of the resistive responses into *shadow* promulgated, publicly manipulated and "cleanly" natural responses free of ulterior motives, we choose the best place and method to invest our efforts with the minimal amount of diminishing effects and the maximum confidence building potential. Essentially, this first run is our "test model."

The *motivation* of the *Sixth Step* is composed of two parts. First is *incitement* which catches our interest and points us in a direction. The second is *application* which is, typically, one of the most difficult aspects of all the steps in that it requires effort, tenacity and consistency all of which are qualities that run contrary to our western way of obsession with instant gratification. The *application* of *motivation* comes from many methods including; *self-talk, emulation and identity, having a sponsor or model, investing in research* and *finding like minded individuals*. Another difficult part for building and maintaining *motivation* is raising enough energy to overcome the *inertia* of old patterning. This is what most of us laughingly refer to as "will power."

116

The *change* of the *Seventh Step* is the actual action we take toward making our chosen endeavor a reality. Its deadliest enemy is *procrastination*. The action of change creates the circumstances and responses that feed the building and encouragement of a self-concept based on autonomy and confidence. As this occurs, *toxically shamed* memories are "edged out" by the positive responses to the accumulated new experiences thereby leaving the old diminishing responses to die out from attrition. This gradually shifts our overall *locus of control* from external to a more internal bearing. As the *change* takes place the most dominant quality needed is patience. Remember, it has taken years to put the feelings of inadequacy in place. At this time it is important to remain focused on what we *do* want rather than what we *don't* want. The changes will occur slowly with a strong attending sense of insecurity since the self-concept will be learning to work with a new and unfamiliar framework.

The *balance* of the *Eighth Step* is a pause in the cycle. It's a time when we step back from our actions and assess whether our efforts have been on target. The challenge of this step is to step back and observe without responding to the urge to quickly fix what our first impression tells us might be amiss. This is much like an artist stepping back from his creation to determine whether it is actually finished or is it how he originally intended it to be. If this work is done with patience, we often see options for adjustment that weren't previously considered before because we hadn't enough feed back or information to see them clearly. This pause also gives us an opportunity to perceive if any coercive actions of others or any of our *ego's defense mechanisms* have slipped into the mix. Finally, we have created enough space so we may perceive if we actually feel better about ourselves as a result of our efforts and endeavors.

HOW LONG IS THIS GOING TO TAKE?

The *Eight Steps* present in a framework much like the eight phases of the Moon which, essentially, parallels the human bodily cycles. The cycle completes itself in approximately twenty eight days. Any minor endeavor that we put into action will usually show results in that time period. In psychological circles it is said that it takes twenty one days for a pattern to become a habit. According to biorhythms the human physical cycle is twenty one days and the emotional cycle is twenty eight days. Even though there seems to be some dispute over the length of time, it still shows that results come in a cyclic fashion. It would also be my assumption that our *Eight Steps* would more closely follow the emotional cycle since motivation comes from, primarily, our feeling and emotional disposition. In light of this it is likely to take one Moon cycle to complete the first run on smaller endeavors.

Other projects, which may be more involved and have a longer range goal, will more likely follow a parallel with the yearly planting cycle; the solstices, the equinoxes, their mid points and the three harvesting cycles. Even longer cycles follow in seven, fourteen and twenty eight year increments. With a reasonable understanding about how our daily and yearly lives progress, we should be able to have a fairly predictable perception about how long our projects might take.

SOME PERIPHERAL ISSUES TO CONSIDER

Having laid the groundwork for our rebalancing, or more appropriately our recovery, it's important to look at some issues that will have a very strong bearing on our understanding of what we're doing. The first of these is that our primary focus is one of replacing an old set of responses with a new set of responses. This seems very simplistic but must be so in order to get the point across of what we're actually doing. The business of focusing on what we *do* want rather than what we *don't* want is the crux of the matter. There's an old Indian story about a brave having two wolves within his heart; a bad wolf and a good wolf. He was very troubled with the battle he was fighting within. He finally arrived at the point where he could no longer tolerate the struggle and consulted one of the tribal elders about what to do. He asked "Which wolf is the strongest?" The elder replied, "Which ever one you feed." The importance of this story lies in the fact that what we apply energy and attention to is what grows in intensity. If we are undecided, we will struggle with the choice until we do. For us as humans, our choice boils down to, "Do I choose what pleases others that I appear in a favorable light and receive their love and attention or do I have the courage to choose what will please me and make me more familiar with what will make me grow in experience and wisdom?" In other words, "Do I *create* a bad wolf or a good wolf?" *Our* primary focus demands that we feed the good wolf. Even more simply, the whole focus asks that we put energy into what makes our self-concept autonomous rather than dependent. When we make ourselves useful and pleasing to others with an eye for extorting approval, we create monsters. We have given away our power. We, then, *make* ourselves inadequate to the task of survival. When we make our power dependent on the responses of others, we make ourselves slaves to them. Those we attempt to control and influence now control and influence us. A silent, assumed advantage, which often goes unnoticed, is that we have, essentially, absolved ourselves from being responsible for our choices. But, we have also given up a very valuable quality to gain a feeling of security and control. That is freedom. Our free will is in our power of choice.

Another peripheral issue is that of *reframing*. Even though our *Eight Steps* focuses on establishing new behaviors and responses, sometimes the responses need to be viewed from a perspective other than the usual way. Coming from a *toxically shamed* experience we would tend to view what we receive from the world with resistance. When we look at a response(s), there is a context, namely, our attitude of resistance that gives it a familiar, personal meaning for us. Much like when we wear colored lenses in our glasses, the color we wear tempers everything we perceive with the color of the glass. The color is what we bring to the situation. The color is a context and changes the perception of whatever we see. Change the color, we change our perception. We can say the same thing about an attitude. If we choose a negative or pessimistic attitude, everything we perceive will be viewed from the perspective of resistance. If we choose a positive or optimistic attitude, everything we perceive will be viewed with an attitude of acceptance. So, essentially, the *First Step* of consistent *acceptance* reframes everything we perceive.

Reframing has its roots with the well known psychologist Milton Erickson and is also an important component of Neuro-Linguistic Programming. A strong proponent of NLP is Anthony Robbins who says, "If we perceive something as a liability, that's the message we deliver to our brain. Then the brain produces states that make it a reality. If we change our frame of reference by looking at the same situation from a different point of view, we can change the way we respond in life. We can change our representation or perception about anything and, in a moment, change our states and behaviors (Robbins, 1987)." We can also apply this reasoning to the *Seventh Step* of *change* when we perceive responses from the world to our chosen endeavors.

As a little side issue, it might also be important to note that there have been studies done where the word "not" or similar negatives like "don't" or "doesn't" appear to be ignored as disqualifiers by the unconscious. For example, to say, "I hope someone doesn't steal it" is read by the unconscious as "I hope someone steals it." The verbs "stealing" and "hope" are what receive the energy. The word "doesn't" never comes into play nor is it acknowledged. In this same light NLP encourages us to phrase a negative in a positive fashion. For example, if I were to say that I don't like something, it gives energy and attention to what I don't like. So, I shouldn't tell a waiter that I don't like shrimp. I'd be more likely to get a shrimp dish, especially, if he wasn't paying attention well or if I didn't emphasis the "don't." It would be better to speak of what I *do* like and feed the wolf that's in my best interest. As westerners we phrase most of our wants in terms of what we don't want. If you don't believe that we are programmed in this way, try an experiment. Make it a point to attempt to rephrase every negative you would say in the form of a positive statement. You'll find that this is much more difficult that it might seem. You'll find that what we *don't* want is much clearer and more ingrained in us than what we *do* want. Everyone can tell you what they *don't* want. Very few people can tell you what they *do* want. It's a very small detail but a very strong contributor to what we receive from the world. Perhaps this is one of the reasons why we find so many unhappy people in our day to day life.

As we follow the steps and begin to receive positive feed back, it's important to note that in the beginning only the domain that we are actively reframing will see the changes. Slowly, as our attitude toward what we expect to receive from the universe shifts, there will be a slow carry-over to other domains much the same way water would permeate a sponge. For example, if our career has felt a shift because of the steps we have taken, our attitude toward doing career activities shifts also as a result of the positive feedback we are receiving. Though we may also have difficulties in our social life the attitude we present in our career begins to "seep through" and our social life starts to feel the benefits of a new approach. The positive attitude and responses that work for the career slowly start to affect our social life. Remember, energy follows attention. This is also true for the type of attention generated, also. Experience generates expectations through responses received and expectations produce beliefs through acknowledgement and choice.

COMPASSION & ITS IMPLEMENTATION

SO, WHERE DO WE STAND?

As we become stronger in our self-concept, our susceptibility to diminishment by others through shame begins to fade. We must also remember that the diminishment by others not only comes to us by what is said or done but also to us through our empathy with what feelings they are projecting. Anger and disdain are very powerful feelings to contend with and if our personal belief and resolve in our ability to remain "adequate" is faulty, we become overwhelmed and coerced by whatever is projected at us. As our fledgling self-concept begins to strengthen, we must also train ourselves to use our intuition rather than our empathy when dealing with people we believe might be of a "coercive" and domineering nature. We can choose to be empathetic if we wish. We may also choose to be intuitive if we wish. The difference is in the fact that empathy is resonant with the *ego* of others and presents an externally coercive influence through the push of its invasive nature. *Intuition* does not have as powerful a push as empathy. We must be tuned to it to receive its influence and must be able to let the empathy "wash past us" so we may tune to the more subtle nature of *intuition*. The stronger our self-concept, the stronger our intention will remain with staying focused with the more subtle energies. Comparing empathy to *intuition* is much like perceiving a flood as compared to hearing music. It's as if they operate in different dimensions.

Please understand that the reason I spent so much time on the dynamics of *empathy, narcissism* and *shame* is due to the fact that in order to feel and perceive *compassion* in its cleanest form, we must be reasonably free of any of involvement with our own *egoic* compensations that might serve to distract us from what is actually happening with those who need the help and support that we might be able to provide. When we are occupied with losing face or preventing others from seeing a believed inadequacy, we tend to pay attention more to ourselves than the needs of others. In and of itself being selfish is not something to be avoided as insinuated by others who are attempting to extort commitments or their preferred behaviors from us. In light of this, is it really appropriate or ethical for us to attempt to prevent others from supporting their own survival due to the fact that all our needs and desires have not yet been met? Is this tendency, then perhaps, due to the fact that their actions or inactions may somehow deprive us of something we need for survival or expose our feelings of perceived inadequacy? Realize that the control over our lives attempted by others is simply the feeling that *they* feel that they have none in their own lives. Like most everything else induced by shame, it is simply an unconscious reaction. Realize, also, that not all those who attempt to coerce or control are conscious of what or why they are doing what they do. Some have learned it so well that it is merely a trained, subconscious response to a felt threat of exposing perceived inadequacy.

In order to work with compassion and be sensitive to its message, we must have the majority of our insecurities out of the way that we may hear the message clearly. Then, no ulterior motives will interfere with our intentions or actions.

THE STIGMA OF SELFISHNESS

As we become stronger in our self-concept, we begin to see things around us that we hadn't been aware of before. We begin to see the beauty in the organization of the world. The understanding that everything is as it should be slowly penetrates our thoughts. As we diminish our preoccupation with our own image and start to release our fear of "being discovered" as having perceived inadequacies by others, we begin to see that everyone else is, essentially, going through the same *ego* struggles that we're pulling back from. *No one is free of shame.* Everyone is dealing with some semblance of perceived inadequacy paralleling the *inferiority concept* postulated by Alfred Adler (Adler, 1927) unless they are actualized or on the road to being so. Pulling back, inherent in actualization, creates a curious effect. That effect is a feeling of loss. It is commonly felt by us but not necessarily recognized or perceived at first.

In the "shame game" all of us are adversaries to each other in terms of *ego* defense but we are all comrades in the sense that we are all involved in the same game. The accelerated interest in competitive sports has made the "struggle to be number one" common and accepted by all as part of "normalcy" in life and, through proliferation, as part of our daily survival. It's almost as if we, subconsciously, accept the fact that not everyone can be "number one" so if we're not fully successful in the daily "competition" of life there is a part of us that finds it acceptable to take our place in the "ranks." Here Thoreau's "living lives of quiet desperation" has special meaning. Our sense of loss is also related to "misery loves company" and for someone who begins to become actualized; their victory is "bitter sweet." The dynamic that this approach follows may be acknowledged but rarely understood. Still, with everything that we gain, something must be lost. The trouble is that most people, especially when we accomplish an objective or acquire something that we've wanted, usually don't see what is eliminated that something else may take its place. Each of us is a little integrated eco systems; a container with only so much room. If something is taken out, it makes room for something else. If something else is pushed in, it forces something else out. Deciding to push instead of pull or vice versa leaves us with one in absence of the other. We can't do both at the same time. We can't be both at the same time. We cannot be a comrade to someone's misery if we have taken ourselves out of being miserable. Let's look at a simple example.

When we are married, there are certain activities and attitudes we do and have. For instance, whatever we do for or to our home environment must also be shared by another. Whether they approve or not will not be as important as the fact that it is reflective of the attitudes and concern that two people share with each other in a close relationship. There are considerations we have for each other. There are things that we do for and to each other in a marriage that we don't do when we're single. When we get together with other married couples, we do and speak about subjects that are particular to those of us who are married. It becomes very much like a club with people of common interests. When we divorce, there are many new patterns that we must develop in order to handle the responsibilities of living. We no longer have a partner to share those responsibilities and, therefore, must rely only on ourselves to handle them. We all know and accept the things we physically must adjust to live as a single person; half the income, one car, cooking for ourselves, being a single parent, etc. But one of the things that is unexpected to many is when we, as a single person, get together with friends who are married, we no longer have the same issues in common. The same subjects are no longer brought up in conversation. The same joys and difficulties pertinent to being married are no longer shared. What we talk about and focus on is different. It's much like a painter getting together with a group of musicians. There are some things that are still in common as artists but the majority of issues that the musicians will concern themselves with are not those of a painter. We feel out of place. Our concerns have changed. Slowly, the married friends we once had a close rapport with have different obligations or can no longer get together with you. It's then that we feel a secondary loss next to the divorce.

The resulting change in our marital state is similar to how we change when we've dealt with shame. When we move on from feeling *toxically shamed*, the comradeship we had with people facing shame issues is lost.

The things they talk about, the things they fear, the things they get angry about and the things they react to don't resonate with our new focus. Even though misery had loved company, there is a bonding indicative of *shadow* that no longer exists. We are no longer in sync with the friends we confided in and shared with. Their mindset and focus is different. If we remain with them, we risk losing all the confidence we've worked so hard to build if we re-bond with them over the oppression, suppression and depression connected to the shame that we've replaced. The positive side is that we may be able to encourage and assist others in their own transformation toward autonomy. Yet, we still feel the loss of the bonding, friendship and safety we felt within the group. It can be painful and lonely for us in the new focus and there is a very strong urge to return to old ways in order not to lose the support and security of the lost friendships. Relapse is always a risk and it takes strength to move past it. We must be patient as we forge new relationships based on our successful experiences. It takes time to find people who can resonate with us with emotionally healthy attitudes. To assist us in maintaining our new focus we can lean heavily into the motivational step where we look for like minded people.

In making our way from feeling inadequate toward feeling confident, there is another hurdle similar to the loss described. When we change something about how we present ourselves and how we work with others, it's easy to work in the new way with strangers. They don't know us. They don't expect any particular behavior from us. However, the people closest to us are the most difficult to deal with. They're used to our old behavior and have a comfortable, familiarly scripted part in their interactions with us utilizing all the "buttons" that activate our emotional interdependencies with them. We must, literally, train them to respond to us differently. They will certainly be the hardest to retrain and, like training a small child, we will have to repeat ourselves over and over until they finally accept that we will only accept different responses. Our past emotional interdependencies with them are powerful factors urging us toward our former behaviors. It's up to us to be perseverant and hold the line until they come around. Still, a few will be totally opposed to "retraining" since changing their behavior will force them to see themselves, and us, differently and act in ways unfamiliar for them. Ultimately, we will have to cut them loose until we are strong enough to feel a "rootedness" in our new perspective.

I have offered these examples in order to set a foundation for understanding a problem created by an attitude developed by others; the stigma of selfishness. In our growing, evolving and the eventual dealing with loss as illustrated above we must also deal with a defense mechanism developed by others as a response to our change. For those who are close to us our change is disconcerting at the least. If they don't possess a sense of self awareness, they will tend to deal with the world through reaction. Those who are prone to reaction are likely to use *projection* as a major defense mechanism in order to be able to deny qualities about themselves they may find distressing. Through becoming a changed part of their lives, we will receive a reaction from them that is reflective of their comfort level. In the above cases, they will feel uncomfortable. In dealing with them honestly, the emotional patterns they have in place to protect their perceived inadequacy that we have formerly acquiesced to will be upended. Allowing us to do this will expose those distressing parts of themselves that they would rather not feel or let the world become aware of. By not adapting to our new focus, they will perceive *themselves* as being selfish. This is not a quality that they will be willing to accept about themselves so they will turn it outward. In order that they may save face, we now become the ones who are selfish.

In general, the accepted attitude, socially, is that we all are supportive of assisting those close to us toward making improvements to their lives. But when those improvements threaten our *ego's* well being by making us look at something in ourselves that we feel incapable of dealing with, that's where we draw the line. The unwritten rule is that those who become successful must outwardly be acknowledged with our approval and support but inwardly we feel jealousy and resentment about what we feel incapable and/or unwilling to do. The only way to deal with our resentment and jealousy is to withdraw from their influence or, if we must remain in contact with them, to accuse *them* of being selfish.

There is nothing wrong with being selfish. If it makes others feel uncomfortable or self conscious, that is really their choice and responsibility. Unfortunately, our current and accepted religious precepts have put into place the social demand that it is a mark of altruism and purity to put others before ourselves and we have been foolish enough to believe them. "Doctor, heal and minister thyself." What good is a sick doctor to anyone else? In the process of growing in "spiritual" maturity, the accusation of selfishness is a cross we must all bear. (Sorry for the pun!)

IS COMPASSION REQUIRED?

Is there a minimum adult daily requirement? Is there a certain amount we must show? In answering this question we must first determine who might be doing the requiring. There are many scenarios which might fit the "requirement" question and it's important to note that those who might choose to respond to the question will most likely make their decisions from an exterior *locus of control* perspective.

Based on the premise that some would see it as a requirement, as dictated by their religious, social or cultural morals, would make those individuals susceptible to manipulation by those who were much less inclined. For instance, a simple example would be driving, pulling up to a stop light waiting to proceed and having a person with a cardboard placard, claiming to be homeless or destitute, looking at us in a needy or helpless fashion. Many of us would just look elsewhere until the traffic light changed. It might make us feel a little awkward but the feeling quickly dissipates as we drive on. However, what if the person walked up to our vehicle and knocked on the window? Perhaps we might give them something just to make them go away. Why? What happens inside of us that makes us feel so uncomfortable? Granted, part of it might be our consideration of the potential danger to us but another part of us has been trained to feel responsible for taking care of others that appear to be "less fortunate" than we. This might be most true of the elderly and "baby-boomer" generation. If we don't "contribute" it triggers our learned *toxic shame*. We feel guilt when no one notices and we feel shame when someone does which is the major difference between the two feelings. Would it surprise you to know that some people support themselves through "panhandling?" Some of them do very well. Those people are experts at manipulating our altruistic beliefs and hidden shame for their own benefit. There are many scammers throughout the world. Those who are externally motivated are the most susceptible. We are only manipulatable through what we want or what we feel we "need" in order to be whole.

In the same light, the "tyranny of the weak" has been a coercive force for hundreds of years. This is true for people feigning being sick or helpless while plucking our resonant chords of compassion, forcing a contribution and triggering the guilt or shame within us if we don't. To feel responsibility for others is severely disabling while attempting to build our autonomy and self confidence. To find ourselves contributing in this fashion is not compassion but a form of extortion. In the bible's "Sermon on the Mount" it says that if someone asks for your tunic; give him your coat as well. This is very good advice to assist those who are actually in need and good training for those who need to learn compassion. But what if there are panhandlers on every corner? How much can we give? Where do we draw the line? There is a need for us to be, at the least, partially selfish just in order to survive.

Compassion cannot function unless the person being compassionate operates from a *locus of control* that is balanced; internally and externally. We must have enough of an external motivation to remain in awareness of the world and what is needed and we must have enough of an internal motivation to give us "room to decide" without coercive influences. Anything that plays on our feelings of guilt or shame informs us that our *shadow* is hard at work defending our *ego*. This is work that should be done in the *Third Step* of *awareness*.

So, in answer to the question, "Is compassion required?" the answer is an emphatic no. It is a voluntary choice we make. If it's coerced, it's not compassion. If it's required, it's not compassion. If we are deemed selfish because we don't offer it, it is merely sour grapes from those who wish it or a *projection* from those who feel self-conscious for not doing so themselves. To feel shamed or guilty for not doing so is only an indication that there is still internal work that we must do on ourselves.

WHAT IS COMPASSION & WHY DO WE DO IT?

Compassion is a choice we make to act based on our having *empathized* with another person and what they are experiencing. It doesn't have to be based on any altruistic reasoning or religious, social or metaphysical code of behavior. It is simply a choice. So, how would we know when to act?

Probably, the clearest and cleanest indication of an opportunity and the need for our participation is a flash from our *intuition*. Since the *intuition* operates in a dimensionally different format from, and is essentially isolated from, the *ego* and its agents, we can act or offer to act with no feeling of coercion connected to hidden motives. Please do not confuse the created impetus with *empathy* which is only the engine of transmission and a method of conveyance. *Intuition* provides a flash indicating potential, the direction that may be taken and makes the choice available. The most difficult task we have within us is determining whether we are perceiving *empathy* or *intuition*. The more *shadow* we have been able to eliminate from our perceptual makeup, the easier this will be. The only way this can be accomplished is through practice. The most effective way to practice perceiving the difference is through meditation. Remember, *intuition* is a very subtle message and our ability to perceive it will only occur when our inner demeanor is calm and our internal and external motivations are in balance with each other.

So, why then would we choose to offer it? Being *compassionate* with others certainly has its benefits. One benefit is feeling a sense of well being when we have assisted another with a task that we resonate with as a result of our past experience. We feel a sense of satisfaction and a knowing that we have been "helpful" by doing a "good deed." However, there is another benefit that often goes unrecognized. It's what we learn from the experience.

It is often said that if you want to learn something, teach it. On first blush we might not understand why, but after thinking about the task, we would realize that we had to know more than just how to present the subject. We would have to be able to field variations of the questions pertaining to the subject and have a clear and communicatable understanding of the many ways of perceiving it. The same becomes necessary of us when we offer assistance to another by being *compassionate*. To assist, we must understand another's approach to how they perceive their problem and their objectives. Doing so will broaden our perspective concerning our own past experiences while giving us valuable insights as to how we may have handled our own experiences differently and will also give us a broader understanding of the perspectives held by those we were involved with. All in all, it's a win-win situation for all concerned.

Since we are part animal, it is to be expected that that part of us will always gravitate toward what will be most to our benefit and survival. This part must be recognized, accepted and kept under constant surveillance. In our history, the denial of its existence, as "suggested" by our spiritual leaders, only served to drive it underground where it could do the most damage by virtue of its invisibility. Although Sigmund Freud was not agreed with by everyone, I do agree that we all are in possession of an *Id*, or an unconscious and totally selfish animal nature. The fact that we all have an *Id* ought not to be thought of as a blemish or impediment to our growth but, merely as a fact of life. Unfortunately, those who are deeply involved in metaphysics or religion don't understand the fact that the only way to become totally "spiritual" is to be physically dead. The key toward living a "balanced" life is to have all parts of ourselves, wanted or not, integrated as fluidly communicative as we are able. *Compassion, empathy* and our animal nature are all present in equal measure. We are a finely balanced ecosystem. Yet, there is nothing wrong with living mostly in one part. Gaining more of an understanding and awareness of one aspect of our being often times requires us to plunge into that aspect without reserve or balance just to create enough contrast to realize the difference between them. It is also important to remember not to expect a feeling of balance if we do. If we are relatively in balance or if we are in doubt as to where our direction emanates from, the only question left to ask is, "Which part is driving the vehicle?" Then we make a conscious choice.

There are times where showing and offering *compassion* might not be the best choice for someone's growth or learning experience. Notice I said show it or offer it, not feel it. There are times we may strongly feel it yet choose not show it or offer assistance. For those of us who have learned *compassion* and practice it, there may be an expectation on our part for everyone else, who is also aware, that they should practice it as we do. But remember, every situation will be different and perceived differently by each person who has learned to practice it. There can be no hard and fast rules as to when to offer assistance. Let's look at an example when the choice may be different.

We all know friends who repeatedly apply an attitude, approach or conditions to a situation and create the same difficult outcome. In the case of one friend who would rather spend their money on play instead of paying their bills, they often find themselves in trouble where services might be discontinued and they may be pursued by debtors. If they are supporting a family, the pressure will be even greater. In times of financial "shortage" they may be inclined to borrow money from friends…you, in order to pay their bills. Being compassionate and feeling their stress and having been with the same "shortage" in past experience, you lend them the money that they need. After a few occurrences, you recognize that their choice to play is stronger than their learned responsibilities and you think that perhaps they haven't made the connection between their neglected bills and their stress producing situations. You also see that their attitude toward taking care of their bills is one of anger and resentment. As adults, we know that the choice between our playtime and the things we've learned to be responsible for is a necessary fact of life if we are to move through life smoothly. Connecting choice to consequences is one of the basic lessons of life. That awareness has come to us as a result of our own learned experience. So, we have a resonance with our friend in that we have felt the urge to play instead of pay but have made different choices. How do we understand the compassion we feel for our friend as well as how to handle them?

There are two variations of this situation. First, that our friend may be *unaware* that their choice has created the difficulty and, second, they may be *aware* but have chosen to repeat their choices.

In the first choice it's to be expected that most people would volunteer their assistance. The convincing factor would most likely be our friend's naiveté (innocence and/or lack of awareness) concerning the relationship between choice and consequence. So, I think that you would agree that we would just inform them of how we see their situation playing out, lend them the money once or twice more and then wait and see what they do with what we've given them. Generally, most people get the message after one or two reminders.

The second scenario is a little more challenging. It is *we* who may not be aware if they have been through this situation previously and had help from others, especially, if we haven't known them for very long. Borrowing to make up what they lack might just be a pattern that they are used to and are comfortable with since they know that they can always find someone who will take care of whatever they are unwilling to do themselves. This is a learned behavior. They may have had a mother or father who constantly "rescued" them from difficult situations thereby depriving them of the lessons that they need in learning to take care of themselves. In this case it seems that it may fall to us to teach what his parents neglected to. We must realize that teaching them *is not our responsibility*. It is simply an opportunity to drop seeds for awareness and move on. Remember, acting compassionately *is not our responsibility*. It is simply an opportunity for *us* to learn about *ourselves* through the experience. This is a very difficult concept to comprehend and accept, especially, since our religious morals *insist* that we owe deference to others ahead of our own comfort and survival. This sets us up for being used by others through our assuming that responsibility and convincing ourselves to feel guilt and shame when we don't.

"Tough love" is where we do not offer assistance to someone who is suffering through a short term difficulty where we know and hope that they will learn self-reliance and responsibility in this go around or the next for the long term. What's sad is that some people never learn. We must accept this as part of life. Relative to our animal nature, Darwin spoke of this in *Natural Selection* (Darwin, 1859). The process is similar to training a child to walk or ride a bicycle. We know and accept that they're going to fall down at least a few times before they get the hang of it. We know that if we pick them up every time, they'll never learn. This also applies to our reasoning and emotions equally as strong but not nearly as observable.

"Tough love" is probably more of a *compassionate* act than what most people might believe or understand, especially, in lieu of the fact that we have had it pounded into our heads that we must put others ahead of ourselves by rescuing them at every turn. It is the longer view of *compassion*. The danger here is that when assistance is given out of obligation, undercurrents of resentment always develop both consciously and unconsciously. Unfortunately, this kind of situation is "fresh meat" for the expanding *shadow*. Whenever we feel "we can't just let them suffer," beware. Our shame induced anti-autonomy training is rearing its ugly head. It is imperative that we don't let the successes or failures of those we are assisting dictate our worthiness in our self-concept. If we do, we become eminently manipulatable by others who would prefer to see us as their personal "slaves."

The desire to act with *compassion* must be based on our clear and independent choice. It is done so we will learn about *ourselves* from the experience. The fact that others may benefit from our service is a plus for them but *unnecessary*. The fact that it makes us all feel good about ourselves and our characters is, also, a plus, but, also, *unnecessary*.

FIVE STAGES OF PERCEIVING COMPASSION

It is true that compassion is either learned or not but how that knowledge is integrated in our makeup occurs in five stages. Much like a tool, for example, an artist's brush, we may know what it is but our ability to use it depends entirely on our knowledge of and experience with it.

The first stage of its perception must certainly be our unawareness of it. To even comprehend its existence we must first have an awareness of people that simply goes beyond focusing solely on what *we* feel and know. The world is seen as an extension of ourselves. The concept of seeing something from another's perspective is totally foreign to us.

The second step is where we become aware of its existence and begin a progressive awakening concerning what it is and how it can be applied. Surprise is usually the first reaction. Conceiving of the fact that others could feel as we do is at first mind boggling. It's comforting to learn that joy can be contagious and that misery breeds company. It generates a sort of camaraderie in knowing that we are not alone in what we feel. But soon the *ego* pops in. The survival and competitive aspects of our animal nature begin to take hold. Everything in the world is not about us, not ours to do with as we wish. We may have to share. Others have a say in what they want or need. There might not be enough of what we need or want to go around. Using our defense mechanisms there is whole gambit of preventative and acquisitive measures that the *ego* might put in place in order to maintain a sense of control, if not dominance, over others. If shame is present, and it usually is, the act of manipulation contributes mightily to the expansion of our *shadow*. Soon we begin to see that others expect us to act on *compassion* as an accepted obligation. The moment we become aware of possibly being responsible for acting compassionately we have the opportunity and may feel the necessity to lie about knowing of its existence so we won't feel compelled to act on it. We also realize that their perceived obligation to their own *compassion* makes an excellent manipulative tool for us to arrange emotional blackmail toward our favor.

Ultimately, the awareness of *compassion* at this level can be seen as a weakness making the scenarios utilizing coercion through guilt and shame endless.

These thoughts may seem to you to be a bit far fetched but remember, we have done our best, with our society's help, to deny our animal nature. In many cases this thought process has become lightening fast in bypassing our conscious mind. The stigma of selfishness is a very powerful tool for our *shadow*. Saving face in the eyes of others is our *ego's* goal second only to our physical survival. The *ego* will go a long way to do what it believes is necessary to maintain an acceptable image in the eyes of others and to prevent the exposure of our perceived shame or guilt.

The third stage is where we begin to partially see *compassion* as an altruistic act. As we work on diminishing our *shadow* and the need to compensate for or protect against feelings of shame and inferiority, we start to reclaim power and faith in ourselves for brief periods of time. We begin to see that there is more to life than the desperate perspective that the *ego* is driven by. The key to this awakening is evidenced by the lessening of our need for defensiveness while being replaced by an increasing sense of self-confidence. It begins to dawn on us that many of the things we have put effort into protecting have little importance in the larger scheme of things. There are still vestiges of the remaining *ego* subject to motivation by shame and inferiority but the pockets of self-confidence and strengthened self-concept lead us to a more balanced perspective and increasing interest in why we are here. The ability to feel that we are more than a reactive animal begins to appeal to us. We start to reach for a wider awareness and to create more of a positive and constructive influence on the world. With participating less in the struggle of defense comes a feeling more at ease and more relaxed. We feel more at peace and comfortable with ourselves as we fall more in line with a feeling of purpose.

In the fourth stage we move past the altruism in realizing that this growth can be tremendously beneficial to our awareness and ability in handling life. We begin to see our acts as developing the potential for self understanding, awareness and how to utilize them. In comparing with the experience of those whom we assist in *compassion* and as it resonates with our own experience, we gain valuable insights into our past, it's meaning for our growth and other options that may be available to us beyond our past awareness. These blossom into a wider variation of options for those we might assist in the future. Additionally, as our self-awareness increases, the effect that the *shadow* has upon us diminishes further making us more understanding of the methods of subjugation provided by our defense mechanisms in favor of *shadow* building. As a result of acting *compassionately*, we become clearer and clearer and our confidence level explodes.

In the fifth stage it's simply a choice. There may be personal investment but it's not to any personal end other than promoting the flow of awareness, ours and our recipient's and easing pain through the assistance given them. Within our approach there is a large measure of detachment as there would be if we practiced Zen. From the practitioner's perspective, we simply apply effort to situations having difficulty moving with natural law due to blockage emanating from inexperience, misunderstanding or lack of awareness. Our whole focus is geared toward living *with the natural flow* and assisting life in running smoothly. We accept the understanding that pain is necessary even though we may *appear* to be unaffected by it. Feelings rooted in the insecurity of those we assist remain unaddressed and the reframing of their situations is offered with encouragement. To the unaware onlooker, our offering may appear as if we are approaching the recipient's situation from an "uncaring" place.

At this point in our reading we have placed ourselves in what stage we think we might belong but we must realize that we are susceptible toward fooling ourselves with elevated opinions of ourselves as a result of interference from our *ego*. Most of our population who has learned what *compassion* is fall between usury and altruism. There is a smaller number of us in stage four and still smaller again in stage five.

WHEN IS THE CHOICE DIFFICULT?

The choice to offer assistance in a *compassionate* act is not often easy and the act doesn't always put us in a positive light in the eyes of others. Let's look at a couple of examples.

As the teacher of a seminar, you are offering training in an optional field such as self improvement. The rules for participants have been issued and you are beginning your second day. There are nine participants and at the starting time only eight are present and the ninth one is late. Out of consideration for the ninth participant you pause beginning the class while waiting for the person to arrive. It's an important subject and necessary for understanding the following material so you don't want the participant to miss it, otherwise, they will be lost in the material that follows. You and the class wait; five minutes, ten minutes, fifteen minutes. Finally, you begin. Twenty five minutes later the ninth participant arrives offering all sorts of apologies but no explanation while interrupting the class momentum. You resume the class. Later, you question your decision to delay beginning the class. You know most of the other participants were annoyed with you delaying its start as long as you did because you feel the same way.

In offering assistance we can never know how the recipient or other people involved are going to receive what we offer. By being *compassionate* toward one person, there are times when this puts others in an awkward and often frustrating position, especially, in their rapport with you. Reactions also depend on the circumstances in which the assistance is offered. For instance, if the person being assisted was obtuse to the feelings and concerns of the people in the class, the response to him or her might be one of anger. But, if that person was either handicapped or had an event in their life that was catastrophic, that anger would change to quiet frustration knowing that those affected couldn't really say much in defense of their own comfort and convenience and in some case may feel pressured to contribute to the *compassionate* action. The receiver may also have had attention seeking motives which would be felt by all and responded to even more vehemently. The point that I'm making is that we can never truly know if what we are offering is in the best interest of all concerned. The decision making process must be an individual one and be free of any personal motives or judgments other than the decision to assist other human beings. There are no hard and fast rules, only our perception of the circumstance and our decision on if and how to offer assistance. We can also agree that some of the class participants may have understood what was going on in terms of the recipient and reacted differently than the rest of the group.

Another simpler example has to do with timing also. If you pride yourself on being on time for work and you are good at scheduling travel and needed time for preparation, you would ordinarily leave for work at a set time allowing for only minor diversions. On one morning, however, you step out of you home to leave for work and your neighbor is having trouble starting their vehicle. They obviously need a jump. You gladly take out your cables and assist. You also know that this will make you late for work. However, you've made a choice, accepted the consequences and understand the value of your expenditure. Please also notice that I did not say investment. Truly *compassionate* acts are done with no thought of reward. You have no resentments as you are comfortable with the circumstances. As with any "properly" handled *compassionate* act, the consequences are usually minor on your part so there is no residue of feeling or vestige of resistance. If there is no attachment, we can be reasonably certain that there are no hidden motives.

A third example is a bit "heavier" and the consequences are a lot dearer making our decision to assist questionable to us after the fact. We come across an automobile accident. A car is burning and someone is unconscious in the front seat. We pull the person from the burning car and find that they are not breathing. We administer CPR. They begin to breathe on their own and soon they are whisked away by arriving EMT personnel. An officer on the scene takes our information and we are on our way. A few weeks later we receive a subpoena in the mail summoning us to a court date to determine a suit brought against us for bodily damage to the individual we assisted. We begin to regret our decision to assist. But we know, in "good conscience," that if we hadn't, we would have felt bad about ourselves for leaving someone in a life and death situation that would surely have burned to death if we did not assist. There are many people who find themselves in this kind of situation and it makes us hesitant to participate in just such an event for fear of possible backlash. There are no "pat" answers about when to offer or not. We must rely heavily on our consciousness and awareness while keeping a clear channel to our *intuition*. There are no right or wrong answers for dealing with these kinds of events. Just be aware that the consequences can be straight forward or very convoluted. Sometimes, reframing is all that is available to us and sometimes a good lawyer. It's important to let our *consciousness* be our guide not our conscience. Our consciousness exists in the moment and our conscience often has contingencies and uncomfortable memories that may influence our decisions. Balancing the relationship with being in the moment and past experience can be a very challenging and it is often very difficult to let go of resentments or hard feelings if the result doesn't turn out to be in our best interest or those whom we assisted.

THE ROAD TO ACTUALIZATION

One of the most powerful understandings to be had about *compassion* is that acting on it presents an opportunity for us to confront issues about ourselves which we, otherwise, would allow to, more likely than not, remain buried within us. It is a vehicle for awareness about ourselves and the patterns and behaviors we have learned to live our lives by. It shows us what we are limited by. It allows us to see alternate ways for handling the circumstances that these behaviors were originally put in place to handle. It lets us know how much more we are capable of. In order for us to evolve we must move past these behaviors and the imagined sense of security they promise us. The *Way* to awareness is to strip away the beliefs that we think will preserve our lives as we know them. To evolve, life can't remain the way we know it. Lao Tzo, the author of the Tao Te Ching, says, "The Way is gained by daily loss." (Lao Tzu, 604 BC) For those who pursue a life filled with mercy and *compassion*, this is most certainly the case, especially, for those who no longer value, above all else, our animal instinct and desire for control and possessions. We cannot truly be *compassionate* if we are driven by the *ego*; only opportunistic. Yet, there remains the need to be healthy enough to be *able* to offer. So the *basic* needs of our animal nature must be sated if we are to be effective in administering mercy and *compassion*. Some may argue that there are things worth dying for. I cannot disagree. There in lays a very thin line balancing our life with the welfare of others. Only the individual can choose where to draw that line. It has to be different for everyone.

PSYCHOLOGICAL PERSPECTIVES & EXTREME REACTIONS

There are situations where the shame and inferiority quotient is so high that it captures the attention of the casual onlooker not to mention the professional. The ensuing behaviors exhibit many aberrations that appear to be generated from a multitude of causes but what we must remember is that the coping mechanisms used by those afflicted seem the "natural thing to do" to them in the face of the perceived adversity that they encounter. The number of issues being compensated for may appear to be diversely generated also; however, it all reduces to our self-perception and how we decide to view and defend ourselves, hence, the implementation of our defense mechanisms. That view can be one of worth or shame. The fact that we may feel differently through varying domains is not as important as how we have *decided* to feel about ourselves and how we proceed from there. Many professionals will be repulsed by the idea that so many ailments could be the result of something so simple and so straight forward as shame and rightly so. How the *ego* has coped with it and its many apparent faces is a subject of wide interest and diversity. But the fact remains that our starting point for how we behave has always to be one of how we feel. If we feel worthy, we behave one way. If we don't, another.

Those of you of a scientific bent or clinical perspective may rest easy as I am not claiming that all mental difficulties emanate from our feelings of worth but there are quite a few ailments and their variations that do. The question remaining to be answered is whether or not there is enough awareness in the individual possessed of them to be able to recognize their difficulties and take steps to correct them or must they seek "outside" help? More often than not, when they get to the point of the following difficulties, help is needed.

The information used to classify these disorders as mental illnesses comes from a manual put out by the APA called "Diagnostic and Statistical Manual of Mental Disorders (DSM-IV)." Essentially, it is a book describing each disorder and giving a list of symptoms of which a certain number of each list must be present in order to qualify as being a "correct" diagnosis. Many disorders, in turn, have many variations all having their own contingencies for proper classification. To the layman, this book may be extremely confusing. However, to gain acceptance as a science over the years, psychology has had to "prove" itself through "evidence based" information much like nature studies have developed a ladder of labels assigning organisms to different categories defined by genus, species, phylum, etc. For the physical sciences, this works eminently well. Psychology, however, does not have physical characteristics to diagnose or classify except through observable behavior. Even in that it is very much dependent on the interpretation of the observer which we know can differ greatly simply by virtue of the fact that people perceive the world and each other differently. My aim is not to disqualify the way the following disorders are discriminated but to show that the causes of the symptoms observed often come from only a few similar circumstances. Since the psychology of personality is mostly an intangible discipline, perhaps following an allopathic medical model of eliminating only recognized and delineated symptoms is not the best approach.

The idea of "normal" is, at best, a fluid and changeable assertion depending on the current socially acceptable standards for what is commonly accepted as appropriate. An amusing, though poignant, illustration might be that of a "normal" person observing a psychiatric ward. The "normal" person entering knows that there is a larger world outside the facility who has agreed that the behaviors of those hospitalized in the ward are "abnormal." However, from the perspective of the persons in the ward, the observer is the "abnormal" one. The perception of illness is truly in the eye of the beholder. We must then ask which beholder has the larger majority.

It should be understood that the following disorders are, partially, extreme reactions to maladapted childhood experiences with abuse or neglect tendered by their caretakers and role models as being the major cause of their perceived inferiority and *toxic shame*. The abuse and neglect may vary in intensity as might the individual's reactions to them. However, some individuals are born with enough psychic integrity and will power as to be able to fend off most of the "assault" leaving them with a solid self-concept. Others may not. In either case, the cause of which choice takes place may be seen as being the result of DNA characteristics and chemical makeup or simply intra-uterine nutrition and experience. Tremendous research has been done within the nine month gestation period leaving us with the understanding that there are many more factors involved in our physiological and psychological formation than just biological considerations.

BORDERLINE PERSONALITY DISORDER
& POSTTRAUMATIC STRESS DISORDER

Borderline Personality Disorder, also know as BPD (not to be confused with Bi-Polar Disorder), has been described as a chaotic and unstable approach toward interpersonal relationships that includes variations between the extremes of idealizing and demonizing the characteristics of others (splitting). The rapport between the person "disordered" and the persons related to is often reframed into a perspective that either perceives what is heard as a compliment or a slight. In some cases the response from others is seen as an outright attack. In either case, the response is taken "personally" and reacted to as a reflection of their self perceived worth. On the outset, this seems to indicate preponderance toward an external *locus of control* which would be in line for suggesting a *toxic shame* influence. Let's first take a look at what the DSM-IV-TR lists as criteria for classifying a behavior as Borderline.

Diagnostic criteria for 301.83 Borderline Personality Disorder

A pervasive pattern of instability of interpersonal relationships, self-image and affects, and marked impulsivity beginning by early childhood and present in variety of contexts, as indicated by five (or more) of the following:

(1) frantic effort to avoid real or imagined abandonment.
(2) a pattern of unstable and intense interpersonal relationships characterized by alternating between extremes of idealization and devaluation. **Note:** Do not include suicidal or self-mutilating behavior covered in Criterion 5.
(3) identity disturbance: markedly and persistently unstable self-image or sense of self
(4) impulsivity in at least two areas that are potentially self-damaging (e.g., spending, sex, substance abuse, reckless driving, binge eating). **Note:** Do not include suicidal or self-mutilating behavior covered in Criterion 5.
(5) recurrent suicidal behavior, gestures, or threats, or self-mutilating behavior
(6) affective instability due to are marked reactivity of mood (e.g., intense episodic dysphoria, irritability, or anxiety usually lasting a few hours and only rarely more than a few days)
(7) chronic feelings of emptiness
(8) inappropriate, intense anger or difficulty controlling anger (e.g., frequent displays of temper, constant anger, recurrent physical fights)
(9) transient, stress-related paranoid ideation or severe dissociative symptoms

The first observation I'd like to point out is that the symptoms do, obviously, point out a difficulty in adjusting to changing life circumstances. They are observable reactions exposing the difficulty the individual is feeling in handling their experience. However, as such, they are only indicators of their struggle in attempting to find ways to re-establish their physical and emotional homeostasis. In varying degrees, we do this every day as we are presented with life's changes. But when the reactions are observed as having an exaggerated intensity that goes well beyond what we normally feel would be appropriate for the given situation, we then ask a question. What problem handling mechanism within the individual is out of alignment with what we expect? What did they miss getting in their early training that most of us gained more of enabling us to handle circumstantial changes in an expected manner? We all make judgments about what is to be considered "normal" based on our combined and consensual experience. It's human nature to want to assert that we are the "normal" ones.

The second observation I'd like to point out is that when there is an observable recent traumatic event in an individual's life, such as a loss of a loved one or an accident that creates a physical handicap, we tend to make allowances for aberrations in their behavior because we can imagine ourselves in the same situations and understand how coping with such an event could be so radically unbalancing for them. In short, we can empathize, or at the least sympathize, with what they are going through. Hence, we then *expect* extreme reactions.

In the context of an observable traumatic event, these reactions are often accepted as normal. However, what if the event occurred in the individual's distance past? And what if upon meeting the individual we are unaware of that distant event? We see their reactions to an unobserved event with just as much volatility as those connected to an observable one. Without awareness about their history, what will we make of their extreme behavior? There is no observable event that we may empathize with. In this context we will most likely assert to ourselves that "there is something wrong with them."

Let's go a step further. Suppose that the unobserved event was not just one but a series of many unobserved events? With repetition, their reactions and resulting behaviors will, most likely, have become more deeply rooted. The behaviors presented by them are coping or defense mechanisms which, through repeated crisis, have become a natural and familiar way for them to function. The difficulty becomes visible when they attempt to socialize with others and are unable to create a stable rapport in their relationships. It is then that their behaviors are seen by others as irrational and unpredictable. Yet, to them these patterns are normal. We then have to ask ourselves, were we to have a similar history, would we react in a similar manner? Perhaps, depending on whether we developed coping skills or defense mechanisms when we were raised.

One more note before we look at the missing element. It is said that the onset of BPD usually occurs during adolescence and young adulthood. One only has to realize that the onset of puberty and our emerging need to develop new socials skills are radically affected by the added pressure generated by our emerging hormones. Many would also agree that this is could be considered a crisis period in light of the fact that the individual going through puberty is now in limbo between no longer being considered a child and not yet being accepted as an adult. It would make sense, then, that these behaviors would start to become visible *after* puberty began and permeate this undefined transition period. It would also explain why many of the behaviors exhibited during adolescence are not recognized as BPD but simply as an adolescent phase of adjusting. But when upon emerging into young adulthood the individual still exhibits what is considered irrational behavior attributed to adolescence, we then start to perceive the remaining difficulties in social adjustment. It would appear that adolescence seems to mask the onset of BPD. But why, then, would most of us still fare well in learning these skills and others find it much more difficult if not impossible? The key lies within our feelings of worthiness and self-confidence developed long before puberty.

To understand this or, better yet, to empathize with this from the perspective of the individual's context within their environment, I have to ask a few questions. But first, I have to set the stage.

You're seven years old. You've just endured a divorce or separation and now live in a single parent family. You have a brother and a sister. There are three of you for your parent to support and take care of. Your parent is now more stressed having to do what was formerly done by two. Not only are you left with one parent but are suffering the loss of the other. There is a feeling of abandonment and loss that's beyond your control to do anything about. You begin to wonder if it's your fault that the parent left. You wish that somebody would hug you and mean it. You start to believe that there is something wrong or bad about you. When you seek attention from the remaining parent, they tell you later because now they have to…. When you behave the way you're told to, you're ignored. When you misbehave, you are beaten and punished. When you voice what you think, you're either ignored, interrupted by your brother and sister or you're told that you're just a kid and you don't know anything. When your brother or sister torments you, you're told not to complain or ask what you did to make them hurt you. When you achieve

B's on your school report card you're asked why you didn't get A's. At every turn you are diminished, invalidated, punished or vented on due to parental and sibling stresses. Now the questions; how do you feel about yourself? Do you think you have value? Do you like yourself? Do you feel supported? Do you feel as "good" as everyone else? Do you feel ashamed that others are smarter or more able than you? Do you trust anyone enough to confide in them? What image will you present to the world? What will you do to hide the parts of you that you feel ashamed of? What are you now motivated by? What will you do and how far will you go to escape these feelings about yourself?

At this point, please return to the diagnostic criteria for BPD and reread all the symptoms except for criterion number five. Do you think that *toxic shame* could *not* be a major contributing cause to the symptoms exhibited by a diagnosed borderline? Let's also return to the issue of trauma. The trail of this child's experiences may not be classified as a traumatic event, yet, the sustained assault on their self-concept will certainly show some of the effects of one. If we add physical or sexual abuse, we can, additionally, most certainly see the possibility of viewing this child's feelings and reactions as Posttraumatic Stress Disorder (PTSD). Let's take a look at what the DSM-IV-TR lists as criteria for classifying a behavior as PTSD.

Diagnostic criteria for 309.81 Posttraumatic Stress Disorder

A. The person has been exposed to a traumatic event in which both of the following were present:
   1. the person experienced, witnessed, or was confronted with an event or events that involved actual or threatened death or serious injury, or a threat to the physical integrity of self or others
   2. the person's response involved intense fear, helplessness, or horror. **Note:** in children, this may be expressed instead by disorganized or agitated behavior
B. The traumatic event is persistently reexperienced in one (or more) of the following ways:
   1. recurrent and intrusive distressing recollections of the event, including images, thoughts, or perceptions. **Note:** In young children, repetitive play may occur in which themes or aspects of the trauma are expressed.
   2. recurrent distressing dreams of the event. **Note:** In children, there may be frightening dreams without recognizable content.
   3. acting or feeling as if the traumatic event were reoccurring (includes a sense of reliving the experience, illusions, hallucinations, and dissociative flashback episodes, including

those that occur on waking or when intoxicated). **Note:** In young children, trauma-specific re-enactment may occur.

    4.   intense psychological stress at exposure to internal or external cues that symbolize or resemble an aspect of the traumatic event

C.   Persistent avoidance of stimuli associated with the trauma and numbing of general responsiveness (not present before the trauma), as indicated by three (or more) of the following:

    1.   efforts to avoid thoughts, feelings, or conversations associated with the trauma
    2.   efforts to avoid activities, places or people that arouse recollections of the trauma
    3.   inability to recall an important aspect of the trauma
    4.   markedly diminished interest or participation in significant activities\
    5.   feeling of detachment or estrangement form others
    6.   restricted range of affect (e.g. unable to have love feelings)
    7.   sense of a foreshortened future (e.g. does not expect to have a career, marriage, children, or a normal life span)

D.   Persistent symptoms of increased arousal (not present before the trauma), as indicated by two (or more) of the following:

    1.   difficult staying or falling asleep
    2.   irritability or outburst of anger
    3.   difficult concentrating
    4.   hypervigilance
    5.   exaggerated startle response

E.   Duration of the disturbance (symptoms of criteria B, C and D) is more than one month.

F.   The disturbance causes clinically significant distress or impairment in social, occupational, or other important areas of functioning.

Specify if:

Acute: if duration of symptoms is less than 3 months

Chronic: if duration of symptoms is 3 months or more

Specify if:

With Delayed Onset: is onset of the symptoms is at least 6 months after the stressor

Upon examining the criteria we might ask how a child would perceive the trauma as a death threat since at seven years of age they have no conceptual understanding of the meaning of death. But even as adults, do we have an understanding of death other than the fear of obliteration? We may hold on to an idea given to us by our religious community but, other than that, what do we know? As an adult, are all of our fears rational? Why would we expect that kind of reasoning from a child? So, perhaps, we can consider the threat of death quoted by the diagnostic as a fear of obliteration or physical harm on the part of a child.

The only difference, in this case, between being diagnosed with BPD and being diagnosed with PTSD is the fact that there may be an immediate and knowable trauma to ascribe cause to. And if that trauma is not known of by the people encountering our grown up individual's resultant behavior, they will again be perceived as "having something wrong with them" which has, essentially, come from the same cause: *toxic shame* contributing to a diminished self-concept and feelings of inferiority.

For one final note on BPD, a diagnosis only requires five or more of the symptoms to qualify as BPD. If only five are required, why would the other four not show up? And of *any* five, it's highly likely that they may be in a different combination for each person. This would tend to imply that the illness has not fully been defined and that there are variations in its appearance that are still a mystery. This reminds us that we still have a long way to go in completely understanding the workings of our mind.

PARTIAL & INTERMITTENT TRIGGERING

Symptoms do not occur as just a matter of course. Something stimulates them into action. If symptoms occur we must then assume that there is a threshold that has been crossed that activates a "coping" mechanism that overrides what's usually considered homeostatic behavior. Crossing that threshold can be seen as a trigger. The trigger may occur in some contexts but not others. For example, our competence in work relationships may be strong due to our proficiency and experience in handling work related issues but we may feel incompetent in our personal relationships due to inadequate or abusive emotional conditioning learned in our childhood. Hence, triggers in the work related areas may more often elicit competent responses while triggers in the emotional domain may trigger "coping" responses depending on whether or not the threshold has been crossed. It must also be understood that just because an issue is in the context of personal emotional responses, it will not always trigger a "coping" response. The need for a "coping" response must be "pushed" past a certain point before the "coping" mechanism is triggered. Hence, the individual may proceed calmly with his life until some required emotional response "pushes him over the edge" past his feeling of competency in a troubled area.

The fact that a troubled area may be triggered intermittently depending on whether the threshold has been reached, and mostly not in other areas where little difficulty exists, may explain why some "coping" behaviors, when triggered, appear to explode in the experience with such, seeming, irrationality. These explosions may well be compared to the presence of landmines in the open field of possible experiences. Only certain areas may be "afflicted" with the potential to overreact if stepped on inadvertently.

Another aspect of triggering may present itself. If we still remain with the analogy of the landmine, some triggering will produce an ex-plosion and some triggering may produce an im-plosion. If the triggering of our feeling of emotional inadequacy produces an explosive defense masking the potential for its exposure, it may also implode attempting to withdraw from the possibility of discovery. The explosion is akin to manic behavior and the implosion is akin to depressive behavior. Manic and depressive are opposing "poles" equidistant from what would be considered "normal" behavior which would fall in the neutral gray midpoint area of being "average" and inconspicuous.

If we go a step further, there are individuals who may manifest both conditions, depending on which issues are triggered and when, by alternating back and forth (cyclothymic) between them over given periods of time. This condition came to be known as *manic-depression*. The choice between which condition is manifested depends on what reaction was learned to which issues. For example, when a family issue is triggered, perhaps withdrawing into depression worked best to escape the difficulties. However, in dealing with relationship difficulties outside of the family, the individual may have learned that manic behavior enabled them to cope better with that situation than with depression. Hence, an individual could react to family difficulties, go into a long depression and later encounter difficulties in a personal relationship outside the family and then become triggered into manic behavior. The fact that they never developed the skills to handle their moods in their early years could account for why they may remain trapped in one condition or the other until the situation eased or different situation presented a different trigger.

As we moved into the latter part of the twentieth century manic-depression became "reclassified" with many variations on how to assess it. It became known as Bi-Polar Disorder. Describing it as bi-polar was a good move as we know that the condition will vary between two extremes but the delineation of its variations seriously complicated its diagnosis. The variations listed in the DSM-IV-TR are mostly centered on which polarity was presented most recently leading to differing diagnoses. For example, if manic happened first it would be diagnosed as one type of bi-polar but if depression came first it would be diagnosed as a different type of bi-polar. Still further, both time and intensity became factors leading to differentiation between classifications. As it stands now, there are many different classifications with requirements for specifiers toward even further differentiation. Diagnosis of Bi-Polar Disorder appears to have become an unwieldy nightmare for the psychologist, let alone, the layman.

The fact that shame and feelings of inadequacy are at the root of both polarities makes it unnecessary to determine which polarity was the most recent. The individual's attempt to avoid the feeling, conscious or not, is still quite evident. However, the fact that mania and major depression may also lead to psychosis (breaks with reality) reveals an important difference based on the intensity of the exhibited symptoms. In this light I've chose to present two sets of polarity; one with intensity with the possibility of manifesting psychosis and one with moderate intensity presenting only reality based behaviors that remain with socially "acceptable" limits even though they may be viewed as "abnormal."

BIPOLAR DISORDERS

The first of the opposing sets of disorder is the more intense of the two. The most important distinction of this set, besides the intensity and duration of its symptoms, is that fact that it may manifest as psychosis. Psychosis is the tendency to lose touch with reality. We must remember that reality will be defined by what the average social perspective accepts as being real, observable and provable. To the person that is manifesting and experiencing a psychotic episode, what is unobservable and appears to be improvable is as real to that person experiencing it as the experiencing of our own physical body is to us. From the perspective of the psychotic, *our* physical body's experiences are unreal to *them* and to them their behavior, whether conscious or not, is simply an attempt to escape what is acting in the immediate environment and forcing them to look at and experience themselves in a perspective that is an intolerable distress to their *ego*. Hence, from their point of view, they're just changing their perspective to feel safe. To gain a better understanding of their perspective we can ask, are you always aware that you're dreaming when you're in the dream? It's the same for them but their inability to distinguish the difference allows it to seep into waking consciousness. We must also ask how is it that the waking visions that our spiritual leaders have had appear, to some, to be psychotic episodes? What of Joan of Arc? Yet, look what she accomplished.

Psychotic episodes are the extreme edge in the *toxic shame* and narcissistic spectrum and manifest in a very small segment of the bipolar population. What do we (the average person) have that keeps us grounded

146

in a way that we are able to maintain a rapport with everyone else? How this differs from the psychotic is still a mystery. Chemical imbalances have been used to explain the mental and emotional differences in focus, energy and perspective. But we still can't decide which came first, the chicken or the egg. At this point we can only assume that they work in tandem.

The first pair is comprised of a polarizing between Major Depressive Disorder and Mania. The depression will be where the individual's energy "folds in on itself" and the Mania will be where it explodes outward. Let's look at the DSM-IV-TR diagnoses.

Criteria for Major Depressive Episode

A. Five (or more) of the following symptoms have been present during the same 2-week period and represent a change from previous functioning; at least one of the symptoms either (1) depressed mood or (2) loss of interest or pleasure.

Note: Do not include symptoms that are clearly due to a general medical condition, or mood-incongruent delusions or hallucinations.

(1) depressed mood most of the day, nearly every day, as indicated by either subjective report (e.g. feels sad or empty) or observation made by others (e.g. appears tearful) **Note:** in children and adolescents, can be irritable mood.
(2) markedly diminished interest in pleasure in all, or almost all, activities most of the day, nearly every day (as indicated by subjective account or observation made by others)
(3) significant weight loss when not dieting or weight gain (e.g. a change of more than 5% of body weight in a month) or decrease or increase in appetite nearly every day. Note: in children, consider failure to make expected weight gains.
(4) insomnia or hypersomnia nearly every day
(5) psychomotor agitation or retardation nearly every day (observable by others not merely subjective feelings of restlessness or being slowed down)
(6) fatigue or loss of energy nearly every day
(7) feelings of worthlessness or excessive or inappropriate guilt (which may be delusional) nearly every day (not merely self-reproach or guilt about being sick)
(8) diminished ability to think or concentrate, or indecisiveness nearly every day (either by subjective account or as observed by others)
(9) recurrent thought of death (not just fear of dying), recurrent suicidal ideation without a specific plan, or a suicide attempt, or a specific plan for committing suicide

B. The symptoms do not meet criteria for a mixed episode (see p. 365).
C. The symptoms cause clinically significant distress or impairment in social, occupational, or other important areas of functioning.
D. The symptoms are not due to the direct physiological effects of a substance (e.g. a drug of abuse, a medication) or a general medical condition (e.g. hypothyroidism).
E. The symptoms are not better accounted for by Bereavement, (e.g. loss of a loved one), the symptoms persist for longer than 2 months or are characterized by marked functional impairment, morbid preoccupation with worthlessness, suicidal ideation, psychotic symptoms, or psychomotor retardation.

Criteria for Manic Episode

A. A distinct period of abnormality and persistently elevated, expansive, or irritable mood, lasting at least one week (or any duration if hospitalization is necessary).

B. During the period of mood disturbance, three (or more) of the following symptoms have persisted (four if the mood is only irritable) and have been present to a significant degree:

    (1) inflated self-esteem or grandiosity
    (2) decreased need for sleep (e.g. feels rested after only 3 hours of sleep)
    (3) more talkative than usual or pressure to keep talking
    (4) flight of ideas or subjective experience that thoughts are racing
    (5) distractibility (e.g. attention too easily drawn to unimportant or irrelevant external stimuli)
    (6) increase in goal-oriented activity (either socially, at work or school, or sexually)or psychomotor agitation
    (7) excessive involvement in pleasurable activities that have a high potential for painful consequences (e.g. engaging in unrestrained buying sprees, sexual indiscretions, or foolish business investments)

C. The symptoms do not meet criteria for a mixed episode (see p. 365)
D. The mood disturbance is sufficiently severe to cause marked impairment in occupational functioning or in usual social activities or relationships with others, or to necessitate hospitalization to prevent harm to self or others, or there are psychotic features.
E. The symptoms are not due to the direct physiological effects of a substance (e.g. a drug of abuse, a medication, or other treatment) or a general medical condition (e.g. hypothyroidism).

Note: Manic-like episodes that are clearly caused by somatic antidepressant treatment (e.g. medication, electroconvulsive therapy, light therapy) should not count toward a diagnosis of Bipolar I Disorder.

On first observation it's curious to note that there are no specifiers on mania for children or adolescents and for depression there is only one. Aside from psychosis, is it then to be assumed that these behaviors indicate that it is considered "normal" for the developing child or adolescent to be outgoing but not quiet? Does this indicate that there are different allowable thresholds for these actions among children and adolescents than for adults? This blurring of the lines between diagnoses will appear more blatant when we look at the less intense polarity of dysthymia and hypomania.

Upon stepping back from both of these sets of criteria we can easily see that one behavior accelerates activity and the other, essentially, shuts it down. Both seem to "push away" from a socially considered balance point that enables the individual to maintain a rapport of reciprocity with their environment and the people involved in it. Both the acceleration and the withdrawal limit their exposure to any stimuli that might draw their attention to personally undesirable subjects; namely, their perceived world's opinion of and response to their presence and adequacy. It would also have to be understood that this type of reaction(s) would have to be generated and staged subconsciously. In and of themselves we can view these symptoms and behaviors as combined defense mechanisms the individual has utilized to cope with, what they consider, a hostile environment. We then have to ask what in their experience has led them to perceive their environment as hostile. This brings us back to their upbringing, their rapport with their caretakers and how they learned to respond to their environment.

We can argue that these symptoms may manifest as the result of hormone or endocrine imbalances, but, many studies have shown that any sustained emotional state has a tremendous effect on the stasis of our hormonal balance and the functioning of our endocrine system. All "disease" is the result of a chemical predisposition (hereditary) combined with emotional triggers (environment). This perspective nullifies the conflict between "nature vs. nurture." Each contributes to the creation of the other; yet, both are required for the manifestation of balance *and* imbalance. Our social judgment of acceptable health and behavior determines which is which.

On a special note, one of the major contributors to the predisposition of our hereditary health is widely neglected and ignored as having any major effect on our behavior except for some minor consideration for individuals who still reside in the womb. That field is nutrition. As per media claims, only 6% of MD's have *any* training in nutrition, yet, it's illegal to practice nutrition without a license. Additionally, the FDA has been attempting to make the use of supplements part of a doctor's prescriptive responsibilities. I believe the conclusions we can draw from this and the drug industry are self explanatory.

Our second polarity is very similar to the first except for the intensity of symptoms, duration and the potential for suicide and/or hospitalization. These are dysthymia and hypomania. Following is the criteria for diagnosis from the DSM-IV-TR.

Diagnostic criteria for 300.4 Dysthymic Disorder

A. Depressed mood most of the day, for most days than not, as indicated either by subjective account or observation by others, for at least 2 years. Note: in children and adolescents, mood can be irritable and duration time must be 1 year.

B. Presence, while depressed, of two (or more) of the following:

   (1) poor appetite or overeating
   (2) insomnia or hypersomnia
   (3) low energy or fatigue
   (4) low self-esteem
   (5) poor concentration or difficulty making decisions
   (6) feelings of hopelessness

C. During the two year period(1 year for children or adolescents) of the disturbance, the
person has never been without the symptoms in Criteria A and B for more than 2 months

   at time.

D. No major depressive episode (see p. 356) has been present during the first 2 years of the
disturbance (1 year for children and adolescents); i.e., the disturbance is not better

   accounted for by Chronic Major Depressive Disorder, or Major Depressive Disorder, in

   Partial Remission.

   Note: There may have been a previous Major Depressive Episode provided there was a full remission (no significant signs or symptoms for 2 months) before development of the

Dysthymic Disorder. In addition, after the initial 2 years (1 year in children and

adolescents) of Dysthymic Disorder, in which case both diagnoses may be given when

the criteria are met for a Major Depressive Disorder.

E. There has never been a Manic Episode (see p. 362), a Mixed Episode (see p. 365), or a
Hypomanic Episode (see p. 368), and criteria have never been met for Cyclothymic

Disorder.

F. The disturbance does not occur exclusively during the course of a chronic Psychotic
Disorder, such as Schizophrenia or Delusional Disorder.

G. The symptoms are not due to the physiological effects of a substance (e.g., a drug of abuse, a medication) or a general medical condition (e.g., hypothyroidism).

H. The symptoms cause clinically significant distress or impairment in social, occupational, or other important areas of functioning.

Specify if:

Early Onset: if onset is before 21 years

Late Onset: if onset is 21 years or older

Specify if:

With Atypical Features (see p. 420)

Diagnostic Criteria for Hypomanic Episode

A. A distinct period of persistently elevated, expansive, or irritable mood, lasting throughout at least 4 days, that is clearly different from the usual nondepressed mood.

B. During the period of mood disturbance, three (or more) of the following symptoms have persisted(four if the mood is only irritable) and have been present to a significant degree:

   (1) inflated self-esteem or grandiosity
   (2) decreased need for sleep (e.g., feels rested after only 3 hours of sleep)
   (3) more talkative than usual or pressure to keep talking
   (4) flight of ideas or subjective experience that thoughts are racing
   (5) distractibility (e.g. attention too easily drawn to unimportant or irrelevant external stimuli)
   (6) increase in goal-oriented activity (either socially, at work or school, or sexually)or psychomotor agitation
   (7) excessive involvement in pleasurable activities that have a high potential for painful consequences (e.g. engaging in unrestrained buying sprees, sexual indiscretions, or foolish business investments)

C. The episode is associated with an unequivocal change in functioning that is
uncharacteristic of the person when not symptomatic.

D. The disturbance in mood and the change in functioning are observable by others.

E. The episode is not severe enough to cause a marked impairment in social or occupational functioning, or to necessitate hospitalization, and there are no psychotic features.

F. The symptoms are not due to the physiological effects of a substance (e.g., a drug of abuse, a medication, or other treatment) or a general medical condition (e.g., hypothyroidism).

Note: Hypomaniac-like episodes that are clearly caused by somatic antidepressant treatment (e.g., medication, electroconvulsive therapy, light therapy) should not count toward a diagnosis of Bipolar II Disorder.

When we compare the symptoms of Dysthymic Disorder to Major Depressive Disorder and of a Manic Episode to a Hypomanic Episode, we can see that there is relatively little difference except for their intensity and duration and that the Manic Episode and Major Depressive Disorder also include the potential for suicide and hospitalization. We can easily see that dysthymia and hypomania rest on the *toxic shame* and narcissism spectrum more toward the balance point than toward the extremes. If psychosis is present, we will find it on either extreme. It should also be noted that these disorders are reactive in nature. That is, their manifestation is a result of their encounter with the external environment and therefore, to be considered as being directed by an external *locus of control*. We can also see the evidence of abuse and neglect in that their manifestation of the condition(s) is a pushing away of their interaction with others. We can also safely assume that this need must be an attempt to remove themselves from the potential for pain and exposure originating from experiences that might diminish their self-concept still further. In short, they've become "gun shy" and will do whatever it takes to reduce their sensitivity to external influences.

As with other conditions, symptoms of imbalance will also be evidenced in the workings of the hormones and endocrine system. These will be most apparent with the levels of dopamine, serotonin and other neurotransmitters. We must also remember that symptoms and chemical imbalances are a reflection of each other and that they both have a profound effect on each other. Depending on the intensity of imbalance, they may not always be observed but *both* will always be present.

There is another set of reactions to outside stimuli that follows the same pattern of either withdrawing or pushing outward to avoid being receptive to perceived potentially destructive and diminishing external influences. This is Attention Deficit Hyperactivity Disorder (ADHD).

ATTENTION DEFICIT/HYPERACTIVITY DISORDER

This disorder has a tremendous amount of controversy behind it. It is a relatively new disorder, so it would follow that it would get more attention than more "conventional" issues. This has led to it being over diagnosed which has also led to controversy about the extent with which medications have been prescribed, especially, for children.

Additionally, the fact that the disorder straddles the ages across puberty adds difficulty to the accuracy of diagnoses. The symptoms remain the same but they may manifest differently due to the expected behaviors accorded to different age groups. Cultural differences may also produce difficulty in diagnoses in that some cultures are more dynamic and out going and would make broader allowances for impulsivity. More reserved cultures would allow for more inattentiveness under the assumption of personal privacy. However, the greatest difficulty comes mostly from the newness of its more recent "discovery" as to how well it fits the symptoms of our reactions to the breakneck speed to which our society has accelerated. It appears to have developed into a condition currently over favored by the mental health community much like the way the designer clothing has taken the fashion scene by storm. This has caused considerable consternation with the more traditional elements of the psychological field. Following is the diagnostic criteria from the DSM-IV-TR.

Diagnostic criteria for Attention-Deficit/hyperactivity Disorder

    A.   Either (1) or (2):

        (1)   six (or more) of the following symptoms of inattention have persisted for at least 6 months to a degree that is maladaptive and inconsistent with developmental level:

            Inattention

            (a)   often fails to give close attention to details or makes careless mistakes in schoolwork, work or other activities
            (b)   often has difficulty sustaining attention in tasks or play activities
            (c)   often does not seem to listen when spoken to directly
            (d)   often does not follow through on instructions and fails to finish schoolwork, chores, or duties in the workplace (not due to oppositional behavior or failure to understanding instructions)
            (e)   often has difficulty organizing tasks and activities
            (f)   often avoids, dislikes, or is reluctant to engage in tasks that require sustained mental effort (such as schoolwork or homework)
            (g)   often loses things necessary for tasks or activities (e.g., toys, school assignments, pencils, books, or tools)
            (h)   is often easily distracted by extraneous stimuli
            (i)   is often forgetful in daily activities

        (2)   six (or more) of the following symptoms of **hyperactivity-impulsivity** have
persisted for at least 6 months to a degree that is maladaptive and inconsistent

with developmental level:

            Hyperactivity

(a) often fidgets with hands and feet or squirms in seat
(b) often leaves seat in classroom or in other situations in which remaining seated is expected
(c) often runs about or climbs excessively in situations in which it is inappropriate (in adolescents or adults, may be limited to subjective feelings or restlessness)
(d) often has difficulty playing or engaging in leisure activities quietly
(e) is often "on the go" or often acts as if "driven by a motor"
(f) often talks excessively

Impulsivity

(g) often blurts out answers before questions have been completed
(h) often has difficulty awaiting turn
(i) often interrupts or intrudes on others (e.g., butts into conversations or games)

B. Some hyperactive-impulsive or inattentive symptoms that caused impairment were present before age 7 years.
C. Some impairment from the symptoms is present in two or more settings (e.g., at school [or work] and at home).
D. There must be clear evidence of clinically significant impairment in social, academic, or occupational functioning.
E. The symptoms do not occur exclusively during the course of Pervasive Developmental Disorder, Schizophrenia, or other Psychotic Disorder and are not better accounted for by any other mental disorder (e.g., Mood Disorder, Anxiety Disorder, Dissociative Disorder, or a Personality Disorder).

In a similar manner comparable to Bipolar Disorder, we can see that the inattentive variations reflect the "folding in" on oneself and the hyperactive and impulsive is projected outward. Whether they are done consciously or not, both actions appear to represent attempts to escape the "real time" present. The root of the need to escape is to avoid the pain and discomfort that comes with its observation, participation and our reluctance to accept what we perceive about projected image. If you are of a clinical nature, you're probably saying to yourself, what about children who have not yet developed the perception and ability to even see themselves as separate from their outside world, let alone, perceive that there is a difference between them and the world that they may find disturbing? For this, we must return to our chemical natures. Remember that nature and nurture work in response to each other. As one advances in effect, the other reflects the change. So, as a child comes into the world their emotional interplay is not yet in effect. Hence, the younger the child is and with less time to be affected emotionally, the more the chemical signatures must take the driver's seat.

Since nature contributes to the effects of nurture and nurture contributes to the effects of nature, we must assume that the parents of these children also carry the genes and biological makeup that promotes the behavior reflecting with the chemical imbalance.

The reciprocal relationship between nature and nurture can further be exemplified by looking at family patterns and behaviors in conjunction with hereditary dispositions and/or infectious elements. For example, if a child has the genes that indicate the possibility of developing diabetes, we will also, most likely, see family patterns that deal with food, the environment and exhibit emotional behaviors that are common to families who present with the disease. It is my contention that a disease can manifest only if both conditions are present; that is, a hereditary disposition or an infectious source and an emotional disposition that acts like a trigger through creating patterns that activate the disease.

We can see this more clearly with the common cold. Obviously, the common cold is transmitted through an infectious agent. If the recipient of the agent is emotionally and physically healthy and balanced and their immune system is functioning well, they will, most likely, not manifest the symptoms of a system over run by the infection. However, if they are malnourished and have the emotional disposition allowing them to push themselves past their physical limits, then in their worn down state they will be unable to combat the infection effectively enough to prevent being over run.

In the case of diabetes, there is obviously not an infectious agent but a hereditary disposition. The individual may or may not start off being run down, but will eventually achieve a poor state of health by primarily consuming processed foods containing large amounts of processed sugar driving the pancreas into overdrive and essentially "burning out" its ability to regulate blood sugar levels with insulin. Favoring sugar over healthy and nutritious foods also diminishes the body's ability to maintain a strong immune system through creating a malnourished state. The emotionally and physically addictive behavior driving toward the consumption of excess sugar serves as the trigger for the hereditary disposition allowing for the further compromising of an already weakened system.

We can see that a young child without yet the opportunity to develop an emotional family rapport can hereditarily provide the chemical potential for developing a disorder, but they must still have enough observable interaction time with their chemically induced behaviors to present grounds for the diagnosis of its onset. In terms of nature verses nurture, it is truly a mute point to determine which came first, the chicken or the egg, where it's obvious that one could not have come into existence without the other. Even so, why would we care?

RESISTIVE VS. PROJECTIVE DISORDERS

So far we have talked about disorders that are a reaction or response to intrusions made by the outside world that either threatens the exposure of self perceived and believed inadequacies or that threatens to further diminish the self perceived value of the individual's self-concept. We know the individual has had a choice to either obscure the awareness and the surfacing of these beliefs through clouding their environment with hyperactivity or to retreat as far from the potential awareness as possible through some variation of depression. The farthest escape into depression is into psychosis. Depressive psychosis is as far as one can retreat. However, the focus of projection can go much further than just obfuscating perceived awareness of the surrounding environmental threats. As our individual matures in his ability to interact with his environment, so does his ability to project his will on it. This ability parallels a growing external focus through a process of disorders each of which have a sequentially further expanded external focus of awareness and projection. The pattern follows sequentially through ADHD, Oppositional Defiant Disorder, then to Conduct Disorder and finally to Antisocial Personality Disorder. According To the DSM-IV-TR, ADHD typically occurs at about 4-5 years of age, Oppositional Defiant Disorder before 8 years of age, Conduct Disorder before 10 years of age and Antisocial Personality Disorder *after* 18 years of age. Each disorder has a further expanded awareness, involvement and interaction with participants in their environment. ADHD is still focused on the self but expands the self into the environment, essentially, without acknowledging its external participants. Oppositional Defiant Disorder takes the first step in acknowledging an external influence through its directed resistance toward it.

OPPOSITIONAL DEFIANT DISORDER

The DSM-IV-TR quotes Oppositional Defiant Disorder as "a recurrent pattern of negativistic; defiant, disobedient, and hostile behavior toward authority figures." This implies an external source attempting to assert its will over the individual and the necessity of directing their preferences outward. Additionally, in relation to its sequentiality in our spectrum of evolution, even the DSM-IV-TR states "In a significant proportion of cases, Oppositional Defiant Disorder is a developmental antecedent to Conduct Disorder." Let's look at the criteria for diagnoses.

Diagnostic criteria for 313.81 Oppositional Defiant Disorder

A. pattern of negativistic, hostile and defiant behavior lasting at least 6 months, during which four (or more) of the following are present:

   (1) often loses temper
   (2) often argues with adults
   (3) often actively defies or refuses to comply with adults' requests or rules
   (4) often deliberately annoys people
   (5) often blames others for his or her mistakes or misbehavior
   (6) is often touchy or is easily annoyed by others
   (7) is often angry or resentful
   (8) is often spiteful or vindictive

Note: Consider a criterion met only if the behavior occurs more frequently than is typically

   observed in individuals of comparable age and developmental level.

B. The disturbance in behavior causes clinically significant impairment in social, academic, or

   occupational functioning.

C. The behaviors do not occur exclusively during the course of a Psychotic or Mood Disorder.

D. Criteria are not met for Conduct Disorder, and, if the individual is age 18 years or older,

   criteria are not met of Antisocial Personality Disorder.

So we can see thus far that this disorder is a reactive behavior toward external manipulation or solicitation. However, as the child's experience with the external world begins to broaden through friends, school and the media, some desires begin to develop. This means reaching outside the current self in order to fulfill those desires. With our limited socials skills, though ill developed under the umbrella of oppositional defiance, some attempts must be made to acquire what we may have decided that we want or need above and beyond our prior experience. This requires us to project ourselves outside of our usual emotionally internal habitat. The absence of learned empathy, let alone compassion, will make our attempts seem crude, inconsiderate and even illegal to many of those observing us in the external world. We now progress into Conduct Disorder.

CONDUCT DISORDER

The DSM-IV-TR describes Conduct Disorder as "a repetitive and persistent pattern of behavior in which the basic rights of others or major age-appropriate societal norms or rules are violated." We can immediately see from this description that the child is now encroaching into the space and comfort zone of others and has begun to "impose" themselves on others. Conduct Disorder is much more aggressive than the simple resistance generated by Oppositional Defiant Disorder. Hence, through our newly developed desires and aggressiveness, our child extends their boundaries and limitations still further into the world. As with our evolution of disorders, even the DSM-IV-TR mentions varying degrees of aggression within the context of Conduct Disorder, "Less severe behaviors (e.g., lying, shoplifting, physical fighting) tend to emerge first, whereas others (e.g., burglary) tend to emerge later. Typically, the most severe conduct problems (e.g., rape, theft while confronting a victim) tend to emerge last." Let's take a look at the DSM-IV-TR criteria for diagnosis.

Diagnostic criteria for Conduct Disorder

A.   A repetitive and persistent pattern of behavior in which the basic rights or others or major   age-appropriate societal norms or rules are violated, as manifested by the presence of three (or more) of the following criteria in the past 12 months, with at least one criterion present in the last 6 months:

Aggression to people and animals

(1) often bullies, threatens, or intimidates others

(2) often initiates physical fights

(3) has used a weapon that can cause serious physical harm to others (e.g., a bat,brick, broken bottle, knife, gun)

(4) has been physically cruel to people

(5) has been physically cruel to animals

(6) has stolen while confronting a victim (e.g., mugging, purse snatching, extortion, armed robbery)

(7) has forced someone into sexual activity

Destruction of property

(8) has deliberately engaged in fire setting with the intention of causing serious damage

(9) has deliberately destroyed others' property (other than fire setting)

Deceitfulness or theft

(10) has broken into someone else's house, building of car

(11) often lies to obtain goods or favors or to avoid obligations (i.e., "cons" others

(12) has stolen items of nontrivial value without confronting a victim (e.g., shoplifting, but without breaking and entering; forgery)

Serious violations of rules

(13) often stays out at night despite parental prohibitions, beginning before age 13 years

(14) has run away from home overnight at least twice while living in parental or parental   surrogate home (or once without returning for a lengthy period)

(15) is often truant from school

B. The disturbance in behavior causes clinically significant impairment in social, academic or occupational functioning.

C. If the individual is 18 years or older, criteria are not met for Antisocial Personality Disorder.

We can certainly see that these behaviors are well beyond oppositional defiance. They project into the lives of others in an attempt to acquire, become or avoid specific influences or materials in line with their preferential desires. We can also see that these are pursued without regard or consideration for the rights, space or privacy of others. However, the interaction is still only within the context of acquisition or avoidance. There is minimal involvement with or in the affairs of others. As we continue to move on in our snowball of perceived inferiority, the child's actions are becoming more and more aggressively engaged in the activities and perceptions of others. These activities are slowly graduating to become the substituted tool for masking the feelings and the resentments harbored by their, now submerged, feelings of inferiority. This substantially augments their projected urges toward anti-social behavior and sometimes even extending to the point of playing with the feelings of others. This brings us to Antisocial Personality Disorder.

ANTISOCIAL PERSONALITY DISORDER

The DSM-IV-TR describes Antisocial Personality Disorder as "a pervasive pattern of disregard for, and violation of, the rights of others that begins in childhood or early adolescence and continues into adulthood…This pattern has also been referred to as psychopathology, sociopathy, or dissocial personality disorder because deceit and manipulation are central features…" Let's take a look at the DSM-IV-TR diagnostic criteria.

Diagnostic criteria for 301.7 Antisocial Personality Disorder

A. There is a pervasive pattern of disregard for and violation of the rights of others occurring since age 15 years, as indicated by three (or more) of the following.

   (1) failure to conform to social norms with respect to lawful behaviors as indicated by repeatedly performing acts that are grounds for arrest
   (2) deceitfulness, as indicated by repeated lying, use of aliases, or conning others for personal profit or pleasure
   (3) impulsivity or failure to plan ahead
   (4) irritability or aggressiveness, as indicated by repeated physical fights or assaults
   (5) reckless regard for safety of self or others
   (6) consistent irresponsibility, as indicated by repeated failure to sustain consistent work behavior or honor financial obligations
   (7) lack of remorse, as indicated by being indifferent to or rationalizing having hurt, mistreated, or stolen from another

B. The individual is at least age 18 years.
C. There is evidence of Conduct Disorder (see p. 98) with onset before age 15 years.
D. The occurrence of antisocial behavior is not exclusively during the course of Schizophrenia or a Manic Episode.

We can see that in comparison to OOD and Conduct Disorder, Antisocial Personality Disorder has become much more active in terms of actualizing the aims of the individual. The major perspective set by the DSM-IV-TR is that there is a total disregard for the wishes, freedoms and feelings of others. The implication is that there still is, or at least should be, an awareness of the fact on the part of the "afflicted" individual that others even *have* rights, freedoms and their space. However, like Major Depressive Disorder has a "cap" as to how far it can go, landing finally in severe psychosis, I feel Antisocial Personality Disorder may also go to a limit where people, assumed to have rights, freedoms and wishes, are no longer considered human but as objects in a chess game. This appears to be a form of extreme *dissociation* or *denial*. Granted, this may appear to be a sign of psychosis, but remember, from the individual's point of view, this perspective is their "normal" defensive reaction to the environment. This is the farthest limit of our *toxic shame* verses narcissism spectrum. As the intensity of the perspective deepens, the perception of operating on an external *locus of control* seems to be completely obfuscated. As the external influences are diminished and the internal aims and actions become more dominant, our individual appears to look more like an extreme narcissist operating from an internal *locus of control*. It appears that we have come full circle.

ADDICTION

Our last subject is not so much an extreme reaction as it is an issue that seems to counterpoint awareness. Wherever addiction is involved, it most certainly may have a chemical component, but the outstanding aspect of its volatility is its ability to distract us from what we must, necessarily, be aware of in order to remain balanced between our animal survival and the guidance of our heart. That balance and our ability to live and operate from that point, I believe, is a prime indicator of physical and emotional health. To be aware at that point is the most alive we can hope ourselves to be.

Awareness is something that brings the need for action or the need to withhold it from our attention. Our natural animal tendency is to avoid anything that makes us feel fearful or puts us in perceived danger. In our social existence, this translates toward being responsible or accountable. When that influence grows in intensity and if it is coupled with the belief that we will either be unable or inadequate to the task, we will often find ways to escape. That need to escape and the opportunity to feel "better" are prime motivators for any type of addictive behavior.

To go into the variations of types of addiction would go way beyond the scope of what I'd like to cover here. However, there is one important distinction that I'd like to make. That is, the difference between substance addiction and emotional addiction. Though both are almost always found in combination in one form or another, it should be noted that the physical component adds much more intensity and focus than solely the emotional component. Ingestion of a substance makes it virtually impossible to mask or escape its effects. It is also much more measurable than issues of an emotional nature and contributes to tangible evidenced based diagnoses if only through the analysis of blood chemistry. There are those who may go only as far as to say that emotional addiction is merely a symptom of its physical manifestation. Again, we would face the battle between nature verses nurture and, again, we must be reminded that both must coexist for the disorder to present. Yet, the physical component does not necessarily have to be a substance. The sound of slot machines and shuffling cards and the smell of sex and taste of food are just as powerful coercive agents but just not as readily visible, assessable or measurable. It should also be noted that as a substance or activity interacts with the body, chemical changes will happen in the bodily stasis creating and strengthening emotional connections to environmental cues pertaining to the use of a substance or participation in an addictive activity.

There are two ways an addiction may begin. The first is for us to initially sample a substance or activity due to its reported effects with the belief that in doing so we will feel great, better or obtain a "rush" or some other physical, emotional or mental effect that would motivate our sampling of it. Or, we may participate already *knowing* that a substance or activity will put us in a state where we feel pleasurable effects. Whether the knowing comes from experience or believed hear say is not as important as directly experiencing the effect. It's obvious that after sampling a substance or activity that we would become aware of its effects. If we found it (them) to be pleasurable, we would repeat the behavior depending on how the activity integrated with our beliefs and morals.

The drive for pleasure that produces an internal dopamine surge is a powerful impetus to maintain control over. This hits us squarely in our animal drives. As it is, overcoming the inertia of our instincts is challenge enough for all of us. The mind has all kinds of rationalizations that may give us permission to indulge more than our "sensible" side would allow. As long as we have a physical body, this will be one of the battles that remain incessant. Like the Beta Point connected to our *toxic shame* - narcissism spectrum, there is also a point where the effects of dopamine may overrun our heart's messages where we become reactive to the addictive substance or activity the same way we became reactive to the perception of our *toxic shame*. This point will also be different for everyone and it also is just as flexible. At some point of intensity, it *also* becomes irresistible or overwhelming. When we couple the irresistibility of the dopamine with the perception of our *toxic shame*, the effects are devastating to our self control. Their combined effects become insurmountable for the average person dealing with them without assistance.

As the pleasurable effects of our substance or activity diminish in their potency, we feel the need to increase the "dosage" just to maintain the same effect. This is known as our body's *tolerance* level. As our body keeps readjusting to the new levels, the addiction becomes a snowball rolling down a hill. The physical effects are unquestionable. But, what about the emotional components? What's going on inside?

The *toxic shame* quotient is different for everyone and is constantly evolving. It is difficult enough for the *ego* to construct defense mechanisms to hide our feelings of inferiority from ourselves due to the *shadow* we're created through our *toxic shame*. But when a substance or activity enters the picture with the ability to alleviate our perception of that inferiority through sensation, diversion and distraction, the *ego* gladly relinquishes its efforts in favor of the substance or activity that can do the job with no expended effort or energy on its part. The *ego* can now escape the effects of the *shadow* through sensations, distraction and diversion supplied through the addictive substance or activity.

The key word to the whole mechanism now becomes escape; escaping the pain of the *shadow*, escaping the pain of the world's seeping back into consciousness through the effects of *tolerance* and escaping the awareness of the perception of being addicted. That is, as the substance or activity begins to lose its potency, parts of the obscured *shadow* begin to seep into our consciousness. As this occurs the discomfort brings our attention back to the "feel" produced by the substance or activity. The loss of the intensity of its influence instinctively encourages us to "up the ante" in our use and participation. Even in this activity we are still at the mercy of our *shadow*. However, in this state, it is essentially impossible to do any work involving the *shadow* due to the distorted perception produced by the substance or activity. Until their effects have been eliminated and the potential for clarity has been reestablished, it is only then that the *shadow* might be worked on and disarmed.

There is another aspect of addiction that makes it more difficult to eradicate its effects. The type of addiction plays an important part in that it may not be a substance or activity that is regarded as being addictive.

Traditionally, substance and gambling were the major venues of addiction accepted by the psychological field. It is only recently that food, sex, gaming, computers, pornography and, essentially, any activity that can be "overdone" to the point of replacing activities necessary to conduct our daily life smoothly, has become more accepted in the field as having addictive potential. Obviously, we can use these activities to obscure dealing with a wide variety of *shadow* issues that may surface. Conventionally, the definition of addiction relates to substituting a substance or obsessive behavior for "normal" life functioning. In this way we can also see that OCD (Obsessive Compulsive Disorder) can be viewed as an addiction. After all, it may not replace necessary behaviors but it does interfere with normal functioning by loading an activity with additional contingencies just to be able to function.

We can also view sugar as an addictive substance. Sugar and the taste of sweet is said to stimulate the brain by activating beta endorphin receptor sites, the same chemicals activated in the brain by the ingestion of heroin and morphine (Yamamoto, 2003). Sugar in combination with processed food empty of calories has produced an obesity crisis in the western world that exemplifies the need for an expanded view of addiction that has been, essentially, poorly perceived, if not ignored, by the conventional health field. To perceive the extent to which sugar has infiltrated our food supply, simply begin reading labels. Most processed food contains a large compliment of high fructose corn syrup which is a variety of sugar processed from genetically altered corn. Currently, 80% of additive sugar is now derived from GMO (genetically manipulated) corn rather than sugar cane. Our cattle are also fed primarily grain produced from that same genetically altered corn.

In addition to the activation of chemical receptors in the brain produced by consuming excess sugar, yeast is produced in the body which, when enough sugar is *not* supplied, releases an enzyme that creates a bodily craving which propels us to consume more sugar in order to "feed" our bodily infestation of yeast.

Addictions come in many forms. However, it should also be understood that just because an activity replaces some of the normal functioning in our daily maintenance, it is not always considered an addiction. As an example, we may look at any of the great composers or theorists. Their trade and creativity may represent most of their waking life and actions but, over time, what they've done has become admired by the public. The fact that Mozart and Beethoven died penniless, that Mother Theresa had no personal life, that Edgar Allen Poe had a heroine "problem" all seem to be conveniently forgotten or ignored because what they left us was at the zenith of what we consider creative. Yet, the hippy from the 60s is considered a pothead, the current day businessman is considered a "workaholic" and the struggling artist from the village is considered derelict simply because what they've contributed is not known, recognized or accepted by our contemporary public. In this we can see that the context of a behavior or activity plays a large part in establishing the threshold for what is considered to be an addiction. In the same light, we must also ask ourselves if performance enhancing drugs are to be considered an addiction. The answer usually depends on who "wins" and if they are favored by the public.

The most valuable understanding that we can have about addiction is that it serves as a barrier to awareness and that it must be eliminated or, at the least, diminished first before any awareness enhancement can become effective. Whether or not it is considered a disorder or not by the psychological community is not as important as the fact that it is an interference with growth and a major impediment to diminishing the effects of *toxic shame* and its ability to create our *shadow*.

EPILOGUE

Throughout this book we've covered a number of perspectives and steps that enable us to put ourselves in a place where *compassion* can become the tool for our actualization. There are a number of steps we must go through in order to arrive at a place where we can progress to a point of even perceiving *compassion*.

I've spent a lot of time covering the issues surrounding the formation of the *shadow* and *toxic shame*, not so that we may focus or dwell on it but that we may understand the mechanisms that put us in a place where we end up sabotaging our own efforts to remain autonomous and effective. I have also not covered the role of our caretakers in order that we may lay blame for our inner struggles on those who encouraged how we learned to process that same self-concept. To focus on either issue only serves to "eat up" our energy and distract us from supplying energy and attention to the creation and growth of an alternative way of processing and understanding our lives and the experiences that lead to doing it *with* confidence and autonomy.

I would also like to say that even confidence and autonomy are not the objective but a space that we must learn to be strong and alone in so we may be able to perceive our own essence enough to make decisions that are in line with our own personal benefit relative to becoming aware.

My intention in writing this book was to present a process of purging denigrating beliefs about ourselves through replacing them with activities and experiences that produce confidence, competency and a general sense of well being and self acceptance. This focus builds new paradigms for working autonomously rather than applying energy to the "repair" of faulty images that have convinced us that we are in some way inferior. Compassion cannot manifest in a personal environment where actions are generated by compensatory motivations whether conscious or not. In that compensatory space we are too concerned with our own image and safety and are usually not aware enough to being consciously able to apply attention to the empathic interchange with another person enabling us to act in a way that will assist *them* in moving through their difficult situation without thought of our own reward or benefit.

The steps that I presented in the chapter on the "Road to Rebalance" show the paradigm leading to the reframing of our self-concept. It shows a slow rebuilding of our ability to trust our own intuition and the reforming of that part of ourselves that is connected to our own individual way of interacting with the world rather than the way presented by our caretakers making our responses fit within their comfort level. It should be understood that most of our caretakers were only acting within the sphere of what they were familiar with and, generally, had no conscious intention of controlling or manipulating our response to them. In fact, they may have been acting only as a function of instinct and defensiveness. It is a very small percentage of them who had consciously intended to restrict our movements and responses simply for the purpose that they may feel neither uncomfortable nor exposed and that they may gain advantage over us through the interchange.

In the last section I included the DSM-IV-TR diagnoses of the representative behaviors for extreme reactions to an aberrant rearing. I presented them with the intention of showing that all these reactions are overlapping on many dimensions and that they all emanate from a similar origin in the sphere of nurturance; shame inducement leading us to view ourselves as inferior and then becoming motivated by the need for compensation. Holding a belief of being inferior is the most devastating impediment to becoming successful and comfortable with who we are and utilizing the world to help us express our innate creativity and individuality.

It is my feeling that the DSM-IV-TR's greatest deficit is its tendency to tediously discriminate between specifics in behavior that are variations in reaction to a common cause. In doing so they have made it appear that *each* disorder requires a specifically *different* approach to its "curing." In dealing with disorders this way we have lost the ability to effectively integrate the healing process. What's even more distressing is that nowhere in the manual does it come close to describing a person *without* disorders that we may compare the two in our own minds in order to even establish a baseline for gauging the distance from an agreed upon model representing "normalcy." I also believe that finding minor chemical differences in the body's hormone and enzymatic regulative mechanisms allows the drug companies to expand upon our ever widening dependency on medication to mask the symptoms of diagnosed disorders. This approach never truly addresses the root causes for the behavioral anomalies. Essentially, our current mental "health" field operates much like a person chasing a bubble in newly established wallpaper, eventually, hardening in one part of the mental landscape.

It is my deepest wish that you are able to utilize this book to free yourself from limiting beliefs, whether induced or chosen, and that you may grow to expand your awareness and actualization by using the ultimate tool: *compassion*.

REFERENCES

Adler, Alfred (1927). *Understanding Human Nature: The Psychology of Personality.* ISBN# 978-1-85168-667-4, One World publications, Oxford, England.

Anges, M., Laird, C., (2002). *Webster's New World Dictionary and Thesaurus,* Second Edition, Hungry Minds, Inc., New York, New York.

American Psychiatric Association. *Diagnostic and Statistical Manual of Mental Disorders, DSM-IV-TR.* Fourth Edition Text Revision. ISBN# 978-0890-420-254.

Berne, Eric (1964). *Games People Play: The Basic Handbook of Transactional Analysis.* ISBN# 0-345-41003-3, Ballantine Books, Random House, New York, N.Y.

Bradshaw, J. (1988). *Healing the Shame that Binds You.* Health Communication Books, Inc., Deerfield Beach, Florida. ISBN# 978-0-7573-0323-4.

Fritz, R., (1984). *"The Path of Least Resistance: Learning to Become the Creative Force in Your Own Life."* Random House. New York, N.Y. ISBN# 0-449-90337-0.

Gazzola, V., Aziz-Zadeh, L., and Keysers, C., "Empathy and the Somatotopic Auditory Mirror System in Humans", Current Biology 16, 1824–1829, September 19, 2006 ²2006 Elsevier Ltd All rights reserved DOI 10.1016/j.cub.2006.07.072

Gazzola, V.; Keysers, C. (2009). "The observation and execution of actions share motor and somatosensory voxels in all tested subjects: single-subject analyses of unsmoothed fMRI data". *Cereb Cortex* **19** (6): 1239–1255. doi:10.1093/cercor/bhn181.

Harris, Thomas, (1967). *I'm OK – You're OK.* ISBN# 0-06-072427-7. Harper Collins, New York, N.Y.

Kaufman, G., (1989). *The Psychology of Shame: Theory and Treatment of Shame-Based Syndromes.* New York, New York: Springer Publishing Company.

Keysers, C., Kaas, J. Gazzola, V., (2010). "Somatosensation in Social Cognition". *Nature Reviews Neuroscience* 11 (6): 417–28. doi:10.1038/nrn2833.

Kohler, E., Keysers, C., M. Umilta, M., Fogassi, L., Gallese, V., Rizzolatti, G., (2002). "Hearing Sounds, Understanding Actions: Action Representation in Mirror Neurons", August 2002, Vol. 297. Science www.Sciencemag.org

Maslow, Abraham (1954). *Motivation and Personality.* New York: Harper and Row Publishers. ISBN# 0060419873.

Maslow, A. H. (1943). "A Theory of Human Motivation." *Psychological Review*, 50, 370-396.

Masterson, James F., (1993). *The Emerging Self: A Developmental Self & Object Relations Approach to the Treatment of Closet Narcissism Disorder of the Self.*

Middleton-Moz, J., (1990). *"Shame and Guilt: Masters of Disguise."* ISBN# 978-1-558874-072-3, Health Communications, Inc., Deerfield Beach, Florida.

Morrison, Andrew P. (1997). *Shame: The Underside of Narcissism.* The Analytic Press. ISBN# 0881-632-805.

Ramachandran, (2006). "Mirror Neurons and imitation learning as the driving force behind "the great leap forward" in human evolution". Edge Foundation. Retrieved 2006-11-16.

Reber, A., Allen, R., & Reber, E., (1985). *"Penguin Dictionary of Psychology."* Penguin Books, Ltd., London, England. ISBN# 978-0-141-03024-1.

Ruumet, Hillevi, PhD., (2006). *"Pathways of the Soul: Exploring the Human Journey."* Trafford Pub., Victoria, BC, Canada. ISBN# 1412-092-361.

Scheff, T. J., (1995). "Shame and Related Emotions: An Overview." *The American*

Behavioral Scientist, 38, 1053-1059.

Seligman, M.E.P. (1975). *"Helplessness: On Depression, Development, and Death."* ISBN 0-7167-2328-X. San Francisco: W.H. Freeman.

Vaillant, George E., (1992). *"Ego Mechanisms of Defense: A Guide for Clinicians and Researchers."* Washington, D.C. American Psychiatric Press. ISBN# 0880-484-047.

Watts, Alan, (1951). *"The Wisdom of Insecurity."* Pantheon Books, Random House, Inc., New York, N.Y. ISBN# 0-394-70468-1.

www.wikipedia.org/wiki/Learned_helplessness

Yamamoto, Takashi, (May 2003). "Brain mechanisms of sweetness and palatability of sugars". *Nutrition Reviews* **61** (Supplement S5): S5-S9. PMID 12828186